SOMEWHERE BETWEEN HEAVEN AND THE DEVIL

A COMPELLING TRUE PARANORMAL STORY AND SPIRITUAL GUIDE

DANIELLE CAREW

Tellwell Talent
www.tellwell.ca

ISBN
978-0-2288-5286-5 (Hardcover)
978-0-2288-5285-8 (Paperback)
978-0-2288-5287-2 (eBook)

INTRODUCTION

———————————— ◆ ————————————

Time and its demands... it really is a brief human existence that we live, though we each are blessed to be given the opportunity to live it. Between blood at birth and blood at death we are given a body to live this life in. Our all too mortal flesh encloses the spiritual force that we are, but like a knight wrapped in protective armour, many of us occasionally step outside this temporary home in one way or another.

Like all things, our life will eventually come to an end. But it is how we choose to travel through this gift of our life, whether it is short or long, that counts. While we are all armed with plenty of opportunity in our human form, some choose to destroy themselves and their gifts, while others create hopes, dreams, passions and inspirations. Some people choose to take a negative journey, harming not only themselves but often others. Whereas many people aspire to greater things and devote their lives not only to their own passions and dreams but to making a difference for others less fortunate.

Those are the two options that each and every one of us must face... to either make a negative impact on the place we call home, or a positive one. Although we find that life is unpredictable and control is often an illusion, we still have some power and the ability to control or choose what we do with this life. Hopefully, our paths and choices are guided by the goodness of the spirit but also dwelling within this human body is the brain, the biggest and most powerful organ we have, and we can of course make life's choices according to what our brain tells us.

The mind is powerful beyond belief, powerful beyond measure. It feels, it creates, it destroys. It is capable of much more than we know, even if most of us are not aware of this. The mind also has a spiritual connection that not all of us can see or feel. We should be open-minded to the unknown and the unseen.

Being closed minded and naive could ultimately lead to us missing out on true realities and for many, missing out on closure. Seeing is believing, so the saying goes. Many people only accept what can be seen or physically felt, closing themselves off from other possibilities. Sadly, not everyone is lucky enough to hear or see their loved ones after they have returned to spirit form. Fortunately, I was given this gift but conversely that gift can also prove to be a nightmare.

I was motivated to write this book to share my experiences with others who might be going through similar situations to mine, to help them gain some understanding of what is happening and why. It can be bewildering if you are not armed with the critical knowledge that will empower you to cope when pitted against the unknown. And it always brings comfort to know that you are not alone, that someone believes in you and understands your torment. The sharing of experiences and spiritual knowledge goes a long way towards easing the pain and bringing closure.

My story here relates my own experiences with the spirit world. However, it's not all miracles, magic and beauty. My tale will reveal some of the frightening, darker sides to my spiritual gifts as well and the measures I had to take to protect myself and my loved ones.

After providing some insights into my own life's journeys, this book will present the diverse spiritual aspects of human life and will explore the many ways a person can embrace and develop their own positive spiritual nature. Importantly, this guide will also provide the reader with vital guidance and advice to protect themselves against evil in all its spiritual forms.

I hope to take readers on a journey with me, to discover new knowledge about different spiritual aspects that they can incorporate into their own lives. We will explore the main types of psychic abilities and the various spiritual skills a person might wish to develop further. Every person is unique, and everyone's abilities are unique. Psychic abilities can be experienced in many forms and the challenge is to awaken those particular skills that reside within you.

This book investigates the identity and origins of both good spirits and demon spirits. We will explore the benefits of commune with good spirits and the shocking damage that can be caused by demon spirits and how to protect yourself against them. The book reveals the dangers of not contacting the spirit world safely and gives important advice and procedures to follow that will ensure safer encounters. The reader will also learn how best to recognise any contact coming from the other side because it can take many forms. You will discover the best way to get in touch with your own spirit guides and will gain an understanding of what form those guides might take. The reader can learn to differentiate and develop their existing innate 'sixth sense', and harness it to achieve good and positive outcomes in their lives.

The guidance laid out in these pages will also help to keep people safe during any spiritual awakening that they may encounter along their own journey. This book provides all the relevant information needed to guide readers through both the wonders and the dangers of the spirit world. Your newfound knowledge will arm you to deal with spirits that have walked this earth and also spirits that haven't, and how to tell the difference.

CHAPTER ONE

---◆---

The Beginning

A year of many major events was 1984. Indira Gandhi was assassinated, the Grand Hotel Brighton was bombed, the AIDS virus was identified, recession continued to be a problem in the USA, and the Soviet bloc nations boycotted the Los Angeles Olympic Games in retaliation for the US led boycott of the Moscow Olympics, four years earlier.

This also happened to be the year I was born. Allegedly, I was born in sin. Sin is a small three letter word that defines guilt, and is an immoral act considered to be a transgression against divine law. Significantly, it is not a word that a non-religious person would ever think of, let alone believe that they have committed one.

I arrived unexpectedly into this world, the daughter of a forklift driver and a factory worker. My birth, while celebrated, was also a struggle for my parents because my father was just twenty-one years old and my mother was only nineteen. They were anxious new parents, unsure how they would get by with a young baby as, despite having two incomes, they didn't earn much money. After I was born, they moved into a caravan for a while in the back yard of my grandparents' home in order to save some money. My grandparents would often look after me since both my parents had to work long hours to make ends meet.

After my first year had passed, my parents had accumulated enough money for the three of us to move out of the caravan and into a new flat. It was a rather small flat, however, but it had to do until they saved enough money to move up into something bigger. And by the time I had turned three years old, that is exactly what happened. We moved into a stand-alone house. This three-bedroom house on McIntyre Road in Sunshine was to become my home for the next six years, until I turned nine years old.

I hold so many fond memories of this home, and the many happy times my parents and I spent there together. Despite moving into our new home, I still went to my grandparents' house each morning for breakfast. I usually wouldn't eat unless my Aunty Jenny made my breakfast. It was usually toast with Vegemite with just the top of the crust cut off and a cup of hot milo. I also visited my grandparents each day after school, until my mum or dad picked me up after they had finished working. It was great seeing my grandparents every day and I grew up to be quite close to them.

I loved my grandparents dearly, since they were essentially my second parents, and because they took care of me and I saw them so frequently. My grandad, Ralph, was quite a funny man who always made little jokes, pulled funny faces and provided me with lots of affection with plenty of cuddles and love.

"Come here and give us a hug," he would say. I would rub my cheeks on his prickly face and gave him a big hug. My nanna was rather funny as well although, in a clumsier way. She would always fall over the smallest things, lose her teeth when she spoke, or she would choke on her first sip of tea. I was always excited to see them after school, they always put a smile on my face and I loved them both dearly.

However, I was a rather shy child growing up, and would often hide behind my parents' legs. But despite that, I gathered a nice group of friends around me. To this day, I still speak to a few of them. They became close, life-long friends of mine which I have always cherished. As I was quite creative, I loved to read books and draw and do craft, so school was mostly a pleasure. But at times it took me a while to become confident enough to speak and share my thoughts with others.

As I grew older, I developed a natural skill and love for sports. I started swimming lessons and joined the local softball team. I was also a fast runner and loved participating in cross country and school athletics. My love of sport continued right through to high school. At eleven years of age I started attending an all-girls school, known as Marian College. It was a good school and I made friends with a girl named Leah, who remains my best friend to this very day. We share a mutual friend named Sarah.

The three of us became thick as thieves and did most things together. I will never forget those wonderful days. School wasn't only great because of my love for sports and the friends I made along the way, I also loved it because I enjoyed doing my homework and assignments.

English was my favourite subject at that time, along with woodwork, sport and music. I also enjoyed doing anyone else's mathematics or English work too, although I often got into trouble for doing this.

Marian College was a Catholic school, however, at that time in my life I wasn't particularly religious, even though I was a believer in Jesus and Christianity. We all had to pray each morning. I had no idea what to pray for so it would usually be for world peace, and that my football team would win their matches.

The years went by quickly and before I knew it, I was turning thirteen years old. In year eight, I loved to learn and still loved everything about school and did not have a worry in the world at this time in my life. I would return home from school and hang out with my friends, Carolina, Mark and Annie almost every day, since we all lived on the same street, Mapledene Court. This is where my family moved to when I was nine.

As I was very much a tomboy, I enjoyed hanging out with them, because we played lots of cricket and soccer in our street and we often went for bike rides. Living in this street was one of my favourite places that I had ever lived in, because I got to hang out with my friends and play sports every day.

Unfortunately, when I was twelve years old and just a short time after I started year seven at school, my parents separated. I chose to stay put with my dad, but my sister Erin, sadly, had to relocate with my mother at that time. She was only four, she had been born when I was eight years old. Both Erin and I were lucky enough to have an amazing father. Now my father and I lived alone, just the two of us. He was a loving, kind, and family-orientated man and we adored him and of course still do. I don't think he realises what an impact he has been on our lives. We will forever be grateful for his support and love.

I chose to stay and support my dad as I shared such a close bond with him and loved him very much. However, I couldn't bear to see him as miserable as he was. I thought I would be able to help him recover by sharing my love as he had always done for me.

However, this turned out to be a difficult task, because my father was more distraught than I realised and became deeply affected by the break-up. He loved my mum and my little sister immensely and the separation meant they were now three hours away in a town called Beechworth. He had a hard time coping with the pain of losing them and just couldn't find any inner strength there for a while. This broke my heart. While he was unhappy, so was I. I wanted to support him as much as I possibly could and I wanted to see him happy again.

Time passed and gradually the healing process began to take effect. My father occasionally began to smile again and Erin came to stay with us during school holidays. With the passing of time, he became accustomed to the loss and even found happiness again. This meant that I was happy too. I loved seeing him his usual self, and those days were truly some of the best times I can remember. Seeing my dad smile and enjoying the holidays with Erin was wonderful. That is, apart from her taking over the TV to watch Cartoon Network, which interfered with me playing my Mortal Kombat game. I guess did still love the Jetsons and the Flintstones, too, so it wasn't all that bad.

But nothing seems to remain the same for long. I was progressing into year nine at school when my dad informed me that I had to change schools. He told me that he couldn't afford the school fees on his own and my mother was unable to contribute at that time. I was shattered, not just because I loved the school, but also because my best friend, Leah, was there as well.

We had first met on orientation day, aged just eleven, and had remained best friends ever since. I couldn't bear the thought of saying goodbye to someone whom I had grown so close to. Leah wasn't happy about me changing schools, either, so she decided to leave Marian College, too. However, we still went our separate ways since she enrolled at Footscray City, while and I transferred to Braybrook Secondary College.

Braybrook High, where do I start? This school was horrible and I disliked it straight away... no, that's too nice. I absolutely loathed it. On my very first day at the school, I got into an ugly fight with a group of girls. For some unknown reason they approached me and one of them slapped me across my face. I had a vicious temper back then and didn't tolerate such uncalled for aggression, so I lost my temper and threw a punch and also kicked at her. The rest of them walked away and left me alone after that.

Sadly, these fights became a regular occurrence, almost routine. I fought back because I had bottled up my angry emotions and I missed my mum. But also, because I found some other kids there, who were just as cruel to some of the friends that I had made, and I couldn't tolerate this. I felt I wanted to protect my friends as much as I could.

I hated getting into these fights, but I always felt I should stand up for myself and my friends. Even though I found it difficult to concentrate, I still loved school and learning in class. Unfortunately, I was often suspended due to my fiery temper, which was not a good situation.

Allegiances, however, changed frequently and a few months later I became close friends with one of those girls that had approached me aggressively on my first day. Her named was Kate Martin. We went on to be inseparable throughout the rest of my days at High School, and she became another one or my best friends, after Leah.

My sixteenth birthday came up quickly. I was in year ten, still at Braybrook High, and one afternoon when school was over for the day, I walked to my grandparents' house as usual.

My grandad, Ralph, and my nana, Hilda, were sitting in their usual spots with their cups of tea. I will never forget that image, of them sitting there with their cups of tea, talking to each other and happy to be in one another's company. They were both sitting in silence watching the television with their cups of tea in their laps. I came in and sat next to my grandad on the couch.

"Hello dear, how was your day?" he said.

"It was okay, grandad,"

Then I got up and went into the kitchen to make a cup of tea for myself, grabbing a handful of biscuits on the way, like I had always done and returned to the lounge. I sat down and picked up the Woman's Day magazine, which my nana loved to read every week. Then I felt my grandad looking at me, so I turned and stared back, and he proceeded to say very quietly:

"Danielle, do you think I can move this necklace with my mind?"

"I don't think so, grandad," I replied.

Then he held it up with the tip of his thumb and index finger and began to tell me which way it would sway, left then right, and then he brought it to a complete stop.

I must say I was genuinely astounded and sat there in disbelief. He just smiled at me and went on to say that the mind was a powerful tool, and to never underestimate its capabilities. I nodded at him as he proceeded to tell me that I, too, had psychic abilities and that I could either embrace it, or block it out. He explained that it was simply my own choice about what I wanted to do, and what direction I wanted to take. But I took little notice of these words of wisdom since I was still so young and innocent, and I didn't really understand what he meant. However, looking back now at what he had shown me, it was just the beginning of my life's path. Back then, psychic was a word that I didn't really understand.

These days, I recognise that I have certain psychic abilities and my grandad was right, the mind is a powerful tool. Little did I know at the time just how much. Looking back, my grandparents were where it all began. Paving the way to my destiny was through them. They taught me so much throughout the years, visiting them after school and just being in their company. I only wish I had asked my grandfather more questions about this topic and explored his psychic abilities and experiences a little bit more. Maybe I would have learned earlier how to block certain things out that might harm me.

It was the start of my discovery of a whole new world and I would develop an ability to communicate with the souls within it. What came next was quite frightening at the time, however, some of it was beyond amazing.

CHAPTER TWO

◆

SEEING THINGS

During the next year my grandad had a minor heart attack, which was a horrifying event for me because I loved him so very much. I was so worried but, before I knew it, he was out of hospital and home again. However, it wasn't too long before he suffered yet another heart attack and was back in the emergency ward. At the time, I didn't realise the severity of his heart condition. I thought he would return home once again from the hospital and be his usual happy self. However, he developed a blood clot in the leg which prevented blood flow to his heart. Before I even had a chance to visit him in hospital, Dad called to tell me of grandad's passing.

I was so angry at myself because I never took the chance to visit or say goodbye to this funny, intelligent, loving grandad of mine. His death affected me greatly. I was broken-hearted and not in the right frame of mind. I felt sad and guilty all of the time. I really couldn't let go of someone who had been with me my whole life. I loved my grandad dearly, his death was a great loss, but it also brought about the beginning of some traumatic experiences that I soon started having. My depressed state of mind somehow seemed to attract negative energy, which attached itself to me. The pain of my grandad's passing never quite left me, and I believe this is the reason the spirits first tried to make contact.

Following the death of my grandad, I went to live with my aunty for a while. I had had an argument with my father due to the crowd I was keeping and getting involved with. At the time I honestly thought I knew better than him and thought that the people I gathered around me were mostly good. But I know now that wasn't the case. I was constantly writing in my journal about how much I missed my grandad, and the guilt I felt because of not saying goodbye. I wanted and needed closure. I found a psychic that worked not far from where I lived and arranged to have a session with him in the hopes that my grandad would come through and hear my apologies. I really needed to contact him and speak to him one last time, to say goodbye and get the closure I craved.

That day couldn't come quick enough and I counted down the days until our session. I arrived at the psychic's house, a man whose name was Tom. The house smelt stuffy, with aromas of incense and sage. The energy in the house was strong, and well, I was excited to hopefully connect through to my grandad and perhaps speak with him. I was eager, but nervous at the same time because this was the first time I had ever tried to speak to the dead. It was thrilling, yet nerve-racking at the same time.

I sat down as the psychic began to shuffle his tarot cards. At the time, I thought all this was 'a load of rubbish', as my grandad would say! I never believed in them back then, because who would believe that some card is going to let your lost loved-one speak to you? Well, sure enough, Tom placed a few cards down on the table and went on to tell me about my plans for getting a tattoo on my back and other more trivial things for a while.

It was quite impressive that he knew about all this, but I didn't really care about it, I just wanted him to mention my grandad. I waited eagerly for what seemed like ages to hear the right words and very nearly gave up on him.

However, Tom finally got to the point and said, "Your grandad is here... he is telling me you have a psychic ability."

"I believe I do since I have seen some things that I can't explain right now," I replied.

Tom carried on, saying, "Don't be afraid."

But that was about it! Soon I left Tom's house, believing I still didn't have the closure I was seeking from my grandad. I thought it was going to be more in depth than that, and that maybe my grandad would come to me and say something I really needed to hear. Once again, I was quite disheartened.

My own psychic abilities are now much stronger and mature, they are fully formed. I would say I am now a 'medium'. Now I have my own power to give myself closure, though it took a long time to fully understand what my guides were telling me.

However, the experience at Tom's house had an impact on me and I eventually met another psychic, a woman whom I came to love. This was a long time after I met Tom. She was a mother whom I had met at Sunbury, who went by the uncomplicated name of Mary. Now, this woman was amazing and I was very excited to benefit from her knowledge.

In my very first experience, I entered her room, which felt light and magical. I sat down and waited for her to speak. I thought to myself that I didn't want to share any prior information with her. I just wanted her to tell me all she knew and was able to see without any clues from me. I was learning bit by bit, and I didn't want her to reword everything I had already told her. So, I didn't tell her too much at all.

Mary began in her soothing voice, "There are a few spirits trying to get through to you at this time, but one is very strong."

"What accent does he have?" I asked eagerly.

"English!"

"What is he wearing?" I asked.

"A white button-up shirt and black pants," she said calmly. This was what my aunt had told me grandad was wearing when he passed away.

She went on to say, "I see the letter, R."

"You'd be right then," I replied happily. After all, grandad's name was Ralph and the letter R was symbolic, telling the medium his identity.

Then Mary told me that she was asking the spirit who was sitting in front of her, and the spirit answered, "That's my girl."

This is what my grandad always used to call me. At that point, I started to cry uncontrollably, knowing that he was really there with me. I was so happy and filled with love, it felt as if my heart was about to explode. I missed him so very much.

My grandad went on to say through the medium that I looked like my mum, and that I was smart and that I should never think otherwise. He also told me to stop doubting myself as a mother because I was a great mother, full of love and kindness.

During that entire reading I could hardly stop from crying. I told grandad that I missed his cheese scones and that I was sorry I didn't make it to say goodbye to him, and how much I regretted it and felt guilty for that.

I asked Mary if there was anyone alongside him and she said, "Yes, there's a woman showing me a blue flower dress that you chose for her funeral and she told me to tell you to stop crying."

That was my nana who came forward. She had died twelve years after my grandad, when I was 28 years old. So, I stopped crying and my nana said through Mary, "That's better."

Then I asked Mary, "Why isn't my nana talking very much?"

"She is just sitting behind your grandad listening like she always has. Although she did say you were the rebel in the family," Mary said.

That made me laugh a little, my nana always knew how to make me feel better. As the session was coming to an end, I had one more thing I wanted to ask my grandparents.

I said happily, and sadly, to both of them, "Will you wait for me, and be there when I die?"

My grandad replied, "You can count on it, my girl."

There were also other things mentioned in the reading about my dad, how, in spirit, my nana had visited him and my aunties, but she didn't want to frighten them. She had noticed that my dad felt something one time as she sat on his bed while he was sleeping.

Now I knew that Mary was the real deal, so I finally felt a little better after speaking with her. She also said that my grandad told her he has followed me to every house I have moved to, which was a lot, and that made me smile.

I left Mary's place with mixed emotions. I was sad because I missed them both so much, but I was happy to know that they were together and happy on the other side. Finally, I had achieved some closure.

Before my nana passed away, my Aunty Sue, Aunty Jenny, Dad and I, all looked after her during the 12 years when she was living alone. Sadly, she broke her ankle at age 84 and went into hospital. We were hopeful that she would make a full recovery, but the weeks went by and she caught pneumonia. We started to accept the reality that she might just never come home again. It was heartbreaking.

Within weeks, her breathing grew worse. She weakened at a rapid rate and before we knew it, she couldn't eat or talk anymore. I was living in Beechworth at this time and my dad called one morning at 6am to tell me that Nana had passed away. I was devastated by the news because I had seen her a few days before and was planning on going down to visit again within the next day or so.

Yet again, while everyone else was by her side, I felt guilty that I hadn't made the effort to say goodbye. I was shattered. Although, she had heard me say, "I love you", on the phone, it just wasn't the same. To this day, I still feel so much guilt at not being there for her passing. Although, now I have a greater insight into the spirit world and realise that her final day wasn't ever going to be a final goodbye.

The years rolled on with me having a number of strange unexplained experiences. Although none of these frightened me, I could sense the presence of a soul. However, I was not afraid and I felt at peace with these presences, it was a good energy that surrounded me. Sometimes I believed it might be my grandparents that were with me. However, as time went on, stranger things began to happen to me. I would dream the same things over and over again. Once, one of my dreams even came true.

My sister had broken her arm on the monkey bars at school. I told my dad I had foreseen this and he said what I was experiencing were visions and that some may be a warning sign, while others were harmless.

My dad had a psychic gift as well, but he chose not to engage with it. He chose to close his mind to certain aspects of his abilities. Today I know why he did that and sometimes I wish I had done the same thing.

As time went on, it seemed the older I got the more in tune I became, and I learnt to hold a person's item or hand and gain information about their past, present, and future. Whenever I would touch a person, I'd suddenly receive information like a video about their life in my mind, seemingly out of nowhere, in just a snap of the finger. I was a little frightened by it at first and didn't know what to do with this ability.

I eventually spoke to my dad about it, and even gave him a demonstration of what I could do. I held one of his friend's hands and was able to relay everything about his life from childhood until now, so that I could show my dad what I meant.

His advice was simple. "That's your gift, but I think you should ignore it."

Well, I didn't listen to him, as I thought having such a rare ability was a beautiful thing. I went on doing this for many other people and loved that I could give people some peace of mind. After all, I thought, what harm could it do?

However, what came next revealed why I should have listened to my father's advice to ignore my abilities. The many strange skills I acquired and the incidents I discovered, brought with them a lot of unwanted outcomes. Perhaps I should have heeded the advice and rejected those feelings and closed my mind off to those powers because some of them left me scarred for life.

The terrible experiences began when I moved into my next home.

CHAPTER THREE

◆

The Move

In June 2011, I packed my things into a trailer to begin a three-hour drive to my new home in Beechworth, Victoria. This was my attempt to start a brand-new life away from the distractions of Melbourne's party life. I was now almost 26 years old and as sad as it was to leave my old life behind, I was excited and enlivened by the change. I would miss my father a lot and my sister Erin, too, since she ended up moving back in with our father.

I didn't want to leave them behind, but the reality of it was that I was ready to move forward with my life. I didn't know what to expect when I arrived in Beechworth or what was going to be in store for me there. I just decided to go with the flow and see what might develop for me there. I didn't usually accept change that well as I loved routine and the security it brought. However, in my heart I felt that it was a change I needed to make… you might say it was a calling. And as it turned out, my intuition was right since only good things came from my move.

I arrived for a temporary stay at my mum's house in Beechworth around three in the afternoon. But her house was cold, even colder than her previous house, which had no insulation whatsoever. But I guess it had to do for now. The spare room already had a queen size bed in there, which my son, Cody, and I had to share until we found a home of our own. I installed my TV and a few other basic things that I needed for the time being. It was a pretty empty, cold space and I didn't feel comfortable at all. Already I was missing my family back home.

The first night in Beechworth was lonely, as I hadn't lived with my mother since I was 12 years old, and I didn't like it. Not only because the house was cold and empty, but my mother could be so difficult to get along with a lot of the time. Although she was a great mother and was always willing to help whenever she could, she just couldn't live with anybody else. She had her own life, and did things in her own way, which I couldn't blame her for.

The problem was that we just clashed a lot. We were on one hand the very best of friends, while at the same time, she was impossible to live with. We are still best friends these days, but she was difficult to live with back then.

On the positive side, I was grateful that I had made this move with my son, because he made living there bearable. My half-sister, Phoebe, who also lived there, was eleven years old at the time but she was a downright horrible little brat. Her upbringing had been very different to mine and Erin's. Phoebe had a different father who was a psychopath, and at eight months pregnant my mum left Melbourne and relocated to Beechworth to escape from him and the violence, and to keep Phoebe away from him.

My mother wouldn't speak about him to Phoebe for quite some time. I knew that this time in my mum's life was very stressful. Phoebe was born not long after she ran away and settled into her new home at Beechworth.

The following day I enrolled Cody into grade one at the local primary school. He settled in well, although he was extremely shy, and refused to do much talking to anyone, including the teachers. This introversion went on for a few years.

I found out later that Cody suffered from anxiety and suspected selective mutism. Sadly, I feel this was due to the anger his father directed toward me, when Cody was a baby. Negative energy like that really does affect a child, even if they aren't aware of it.

It was when Cody was three years old that I decided it was time to leave the relationship. I wanted a fresh start for us, just him and I. It was just us against the world, I would tell him... wanting him to realise how much I loved him.

It turns out that today he is 16 and far from shy and reserved. But back then, Cody settled into our new situation pretty quickly. It didn't take long for him to make friends, the first being a boy named Angus Brown. They did everything together and are still friends to this day and then came Brandon Fitzpatrick, who is pretty much like family these days.

After a little research, a house became available on the same street as my mum, so I applied for it and fortunately my application was approved. I couldn't wait to move into my own house, I was so excited. We started to pack bit by bit, and gradually moved things across the street to the new house. It wasn't a big place, but it didn't need it to be since it was just for the two of us for the time being.

Cody was ten years old when I ran into an old acquaintance, a man named Kieran Vicary. I had first met Kieran when I went to a club in Wangaratta with my friend Bhodhi. Kieran's uncle was the one that drove us there and he bought Kieran along with him. I quickly warmed to Kieran. Prior to this, I had seen Kieran around town and he had seen me too, but we never bumped into each other or stopped for a chat.

We both liked each other after that initial outing and it was 5am in the morning when we finally returned home. I enjoyed getting to know him, and I started to like him from that time on.

It wasn't until a year later, when we bumped into each other again that we initiated any sort of connection. This time I was standing at the bar at the Hibernian with Bohdhi.

I heard a gentle voice say, "Hi Dani."

When I turned around to see who it was, my heartbeat rose with excitement. I felt butterflies when I saw him standing there in the bar. It was love at first, or might I say, second sight.

From that night on, we became an inseparable duo. It only took two months into our relationship before Kieran decided to move in with us. I was so excited to re-start my life like this, just Kieran, Cody and I. It was the start of something beautiful.

However, Cody was only ten at this time and wasn't used to sharing his mum with anyone else. Therefore, I allowed him to sleep with me most nights, to make sure he wouldn't feel marginalised. I wanted Cody to feel safe and included, in his own home.

Kieran found it uncomfortable of course, though I felt it was necessary. Kieran would leave the house around 6am each morning for his work as a cabinet maker, in the workshop that he had built. He returned for dinner at around 6pm. I cooked most nights, though I loved it when he took over the cooking duties, since he is such an amazing cook and always made the best tasting meals. I would hover over him, salivating and keen as a bee to eat his delicious creations.

Also, I love how talented Kieran is at his profession, every piece he creates is nothing short of stunning. He is a hardworking man and I'm proud of how dedicated and passionate he is. He is also very intelligent and loving in his own way. These traits are what made me fall in love with him.

Of course, it wasn't always love and romance, we endured many difficult obstacles, twists and turns and ups and downs together. Although we rarely see eye to eye and have many different beliefs and views in this life, I appreciate the soul that he is.

Opposites attract they say. Well in this instance I think that's the case and I am glad we were brought together to start creating many beautiful memories. Beechworth was such a graceful place. I grew to love it more and more each day. It was the perfect place for a child to be raised; the country lifestyle, surrounded by friendly people and the beautiful views of nature. Everything was within walking distance, which meant that my family and friends were also close by. I loved that about this small town. You know everyone, and you're involved and a part of a close-knit community.

Beechworth is a small, beautiful little town to live in. It has become very popular with many people buying up and developing new businesses, restaurants and cafes. The history of the town was amazing too, giving it a nostalgic feel that attracts many tourists which makes it all the more enjoyable for us locals. We are constantly meeting new people. I have been in Beechworth for ten years now and I must say, I have no intentions of leaving.

Beechworth is also very old, full of many old souls and even other souls that have never walked the earth. Let me explain a little about the human soul, which is very different to a soul that has never walked the earth.

The human soul is just plain energy and is regarded as immortal, and believe me that it is. Once the human body that we possess in this life dies, our soul carries on living. It lives on in another form in the spirit world, different from the one before. In this new dimension we regain our youth, the pain that we had in life is lost and we are amongst our loved ones in a peaceful, magical place also known as heaven.

You are probably thinking, 'How does she know that?' Well, before my psychic gift was open to terror, I experienced many good souls that had once lived and walked amongst us. I had my spiritual guides and they informed me of how they passed, and about the life they lived and left behind. This may seem strange, I know, because it was for me for a long time as well. I would often touch an object or a person and gain knowledge about their existence. I later realised it was my 'guides' putting that information inside my head, they were communicating with me.

They would also pass on messages to me in my dreams. My intuition was, and still is, very sharp, because I believe they have guided me in secret throughout my life's journey.

Human souls are capable of several ways to connect with the living, and can be present in many forms of energy, like a song on the radio to remind you that they are there, or in your dreams. They visit us during sleep as our own souls drift off into the spirit world, or when our energy is at its highest peak. While asleep, it is easier for these souls to get through to us, just as meditation or any form of quiet relaxation involves slowing brain activity down and turning on your chakras.

Chakras have the loving responsibility of taking in, incorporating and emanating energy to keep us functioning at optimal levels. They're the energy points in our body, which connect our spirit with our physical form. There are seven chakras that reside within each of us.

The first chakra, at the base of our spine, is the Root chakra. This emanates red energy and is responsible for us being grounded and safe.

After the Root chakra, comes the Sacral chakra, which lies below our navel. This chakra is orange in colour. It is mainly responsible for our creativity and sexual drive.

The third chakra is the Solar Plexus chakra, lying above our belly button and adjacent to our stomach. This chakra has a yellow energy, and is responsible for our will-power and self-esteem.

Following the Solar Plexus, comes the Heart chakra, which surprisingly emanates green. Right in the centre of our heart is where it lies. This chakra is responsible for being able to love, to have compassion and for possessing vulnerability.

The Throat chakra follows, which is a light blue in colour. It sits, well you guessed it, in the throat. This chakra helps us be more vocal and authentic, not that I need any help with being more vocal.

Then comes the Third Eye chakra, which is a beautiful Indigo colour. The energy of this chakra allows us to experience clear thought as well as gifts of spiritual contemplation and reflection.

Lastly, is the Crown chakra, which is violet. Sitting at the crown of our heads. It is responsible for the connection you have to the spiritual world, and what a connection I have had in my time!

Everyone has these seven chakras, however, some can be inactive, overactive or open, which can mean a variety of things. For example, if you have an underactive throat chakra, you might be afraid to voice your opinions. If you have an underactive heart chakra, you'll be scared of love and won't be empathetic.

On the other hand, having overactive chakras can also be a problem, for example, with the root chakra, you may be too greedy. The list goes on, but it's important to try to balance out your chakras in order to live in harmony. With this knowledge, you can now understand what someone's favourite colour actually means!

There are people you can consult to have your chakras balanced if you think they need balancing. Soul retrievals are also a good thing to seek out if, like me, you have experienced severe trauma at any stage in your life. Soul retrieval is a technique to bring part of your soul back to your body form since the soul tries to escape any traumatic ordeal. We need to find it and bring it back home.

At this point, it is necessary to give a brief summary of the difference between a human soul and a demonic one. Demons are supernatural beings who have never walked the earth. Their aim is to possess people and/ or cause torment for us on earth, or in their spirit world which is also known as hell. They despise humans and want nothing but pain and misery for us. They feed off our anger, our negative thoughts and our despair. They stalk us and pray on us in the hope of succeeding in making our life sad and insecure, by taking possession of us through mental illness or even pushing us into dark acts, like suicide.

Their natural energy is very low, even though they are extremely powerful at the same time and therefore, they feed off people who give off energy. This means that they'll come for you in your lowest moments. However, it's important to know that if you can increase your vibrational energy, you can get them to depart and leave you alone. But if you are being oppressed or possessed, you will need the help of a qualified Christian Bishop to cast these demons away or they will remain attached to your soul. Depending on the type of demon that is tormenting you will determine the strength it has to take over your soul.

A person won't always recognise when there's a demon about, since they all act differently, but they all work together to achieve the same evil goal. For example, some demons can disguise themselves as something good to gain your trust. Some people are unlucky and have to endure such terror from a demon until it can be cast out as long as the person is aware that it is, in fact, a demon. Some of them make sure you know they are there, by moving things violently, altering your thoughts and trying to push your soul aside so it can take over your body.

If you ever have this happen to you... stay positive, think happy thoughts and don't let them win, because they can't feed off your energy when your energy is high. Not everybody in this world will experience a demonic happening because they seek a certain type of soul.

How this happened to me, and my experiences with demons, was both powerful and potent and is the subject of chapter four. So, let's get into my first brush with the devil's worker, shall we?

CHAPTER FOUR

♦

Fright Night

One-night 'INXS', a band that I grew up listening to and was very much a fan of, was airing a first episode on TV about their music careers and life stories, and I was so excited for it to begin. I had been down at the Beechworth brewery that day with mum, my sister Phoebe, Cody and a few friends for lunch, and we had a few drinks until around 6pm. Phoebe, Cody and I went back to my house to organise dinner and just relax for a while before the program came on. I can recall I made sweet potato and chickpea dhal for dinner, which was one of my favourite things to cook… so yummy. Simple. Just a few ingredients and everyone loved it.

After clearing the table and washing up, we all sat down on the couch ready for the show to begin. However, we never got to start watching it. As I was quietly sitting there, I heard a crumble, like a plastic bag being fiddled with. I turned around and the bin fell over, and Phoebe shouted, "Who farted?"

I couldn't smell anything then but about three seconds later my ears started ringing like mad. I began to shake with fear and then I detected a waft of smell that I can say was the worst thing I have ever smelt in my life. Rotten garlic with a hint of sulphur. Then, before I had time to even think, my garbage bin flew out from its place. For a moment I froze in fear. I instantly realised what it was and ran outside to get my neighbour, Leon. I explained to him what had happened and asked if he would stay the night with us because we were all afraid. Thankfully, he agreed to stay with us.

By this time, Kieran and I had only been together for five weeks. I didn't want to call him as he was, and still is, a sceptic. He didn't believe in the spirit world or anything about it, therefore, I decided not to bother him.

That night was the worst night of my life. This invisible soul that I knew was a demon was tormenting me and making sure I didn't sleep all night. It was hovering over me trying to make me weak and depressed. It had attached itself to my soul. I was beyond scared.

Around one year prior to this event, my sister Phoebe had told me a story of a frightful night for her, sitting down by the creek around 2am in the morning, with her friend. She saw something black, that she initially thought was a tree. However, she soon realised she was wrong when the image turned around and glided towards them. She told me that it was black with a hood and a white face. Of course, I knew straight away what this was, although I didn't want to scare her at the time so I didn't tell her. But Phoebe began to act strangely after the sighting. She became angry and severely depressed, crying all the time. She even cut herself.

I knew that her agitation was due to the demon she had seen that night by the creek. I desperately wanted to help her but I was also afraid for myself. On a Sunday over the Easter weekend of April 2013 I took Phoebe to the Anglican church to have her christened as a protection. Some might think at this stage that I'm some God-bothering nut. However, it will become apparent in my story why I opened up to this newfound faith that saved me and my family.

As that long night went on, myself, my son, my sister and my neighbour, Leon, all crowded onto one queen-sized bed. The sulphur odour continued to hover around us, above, behind and every side of us, keeping me awake. It prevented me from having any sleep, in order to weaken me enough to enable possession. Now, at this moment I'm sure many readers will have their doubts and some may think that I am outright crazy. The fact is, I too would have thought a person was crazy if this hadn't happened to me. But unfortunately, this traumatic event *was* happening to me. Why me?

While the others had managed to snatch a little sleep, by 6am I still hadn't slept a wink. That's because the oppression was happening to me! This demon had attached its negative soul to mine. It wanted to harm me and eliminate all my strength to make me weak. It wanted to change my thoughts from happy and positive to abject despair. I learned the hard way that this was the aim of its demon kind. They prey on the vulnerable, the elderly, people that take drugs or prescription medication, the depressed and the weak minded. That's because these people are already vulnerable and it's easier to take control of them.

Yes, it sounds crazy doesn't it? Readers may wonder how does she know all of this? These insights and knowledge came to me over time, from many demonic experiences, and my gift of a better insight into the spirit world came with it.

As morning broke, I thanked Leon profusely for lending his strength and his company when we really needed it. Then he went home. My sister, my son and I got ready and waited desperately for 9am to come around so we could head to the church for guidance.

At this time, Mother Bethly was the minister at the Anglican Church in Beechworth. I walked into the church with tears in my eyes. They were pouring uncontrollably down my face because the demon was playing with my emotions. My inner feelings were out of control and making me feel depressed. I tried to fight it, knowing that this wasn't normal for me, but they were so powerful… powerful beyond measure, beyond belief. Although I am certainly not delusional, a sane person might be tempted to think so.

This experience was the most horrible, traumatic experience a person could ever encounter and it's often a battle you have to wage on your own. I would never force people to believe in the existence of such nasty, powerful souls or urge them to take up religion just for the sake of it. I would like to help any other person reading this, who might have experienced similar attacks. I want to reach out to people who have no knowledge about demons, or those who are non-believers who feel they're going crazy and think they must have a mental illness. This is what demons want them to believe.

Mental illness is a common issue afflicting a wide range of people throughout our population. So, demons try to make victims feel as though they are going insane. They feed off our anger, sadness, and despair. The negative emotions people manifest help make demons stronger and more likely to succeed in their goal of permanent oppression and possession.

Mother Bethly led my sister, Cody and I to her table for me to explain my awful situation. While fighting back tears, I began to tell her what had happened. I explained that my vision was blurry, and I felt like something was trying to push my soul out of my body. I was depressed, afraid, permanently dizzy and I was crying all the time. I was also afraid for my son's safety, although I knew the demon had attached itself to me. It was obviously me that it wanted, and it was me that it was oppressing.

This happens when a soul is vulnerable and in a weak state of mind. At this point, I thought to myself, "What did I do to deserve this? I'm fine."

However, there are many ways in which you become vulnerable to these horrific attacks. For example, consuming alcohol can make you vulnerable, because it alters the spiritual state of the mind. I believe that having a spiritual gift was the reason this demon was initially drawn to me, as I am open to the spiritual world and can easily be a portal for them to exploit. I also believe it was drawn to me since I lived near an old swamp-land with a creek running through it. This is an environment that attracts demons, they love to be near unsalted water and old land.

Mother Bethly immediately had faith in me and believed what I was telling her. She contacted Father Glenn Harvey, a Bishop in Wodonga. They considered that they might need to perform an exorcism on me in my home. They started investigating the situation. At first, Father Glenn left me to deal with this monster on my own for a few weeks until he was absolutely sure I was the target of an attempted possession.

Once he came to the conclusion that I was in fact being tormented and at risk of being possessed, he decided to bless my home to see if the demon would leave. However, that didn't work. The demon had taken hold of a part of me, a part of my soul, and it wanted to push out my soul or destroy it, so it could take over my human form. It wanted to achieve this so it could experience what it's like to live on earth, and go on to destroy other humans.

As I said earlier, these nasty beings are souls that have never walked the earth. This is why they try to take over a human body, not only so they can experience life but also to wreak havoc. How crazy do I sound, so far? Trust me, I would agree with that conclusion if I didn't actually experience this horrid event first hand.

Father Glenn visited my house within two days of the request to bless my house. He had a good understanding of the situation and explained exactly what was happening in my home, and within me. He continued to visit a couple more times to see if the threat had left, but it had remained. At this point, I would say I was suffering immensely.

After the blessing was done, I decided to visit my dad in Melbourne for the weekend. I was seeking some sort of respite from my home and the torment in it. But the bastard was there with me in Melbourne, too. It was as if it had woven itself into my soul. You see, once a demonic entity has attached itself to you, there is absolutely no way of getting rid of it without an exorcism. Here I go again sounding all crazy and religious. I have always believed in Jesus but I was never really particularly religious until this dangerous experience happened to me.

I slept in my dad's bedroom that weekend because the demon kept creating so much fear in me in order to weaken me. I couldn't find the courage to be alone anywhere, not even for one minute. I could feel it constantly going through me. The feeling is so hard to put into words. It is even frightening for me to relive it and write about it. However, I've decided to speak up and put it on paper, so that anybody else who needs guidance can find help for themselves. I wouldn't know where I'd be if I didn't get the help I needed, and even more so if I didn't know that demons existed and just thought that I was losing my mind. How many poor people have been incorrectly diagnosed with a mental illness when in fact they were being attacked by a demon entity wanting to take over?

I couldn't return home from Melbourne quick enough to get back in contact with Father Glenn. I hoped he could expedite the relief I needed. I realised that I desperately needed an exorcism. That was my last chance at removing this horrible attachment.

This demon was an instrument of Satan. Yes, Satan is their leader, just as I now believe Jesus is ours. Satan sends his followers to destroy as many of God's children as he can. He is often successful, with some victims committing suicide, some being confined to a mental institution, some having to suffer possession until they are either saved or sent away to psychiatric wards. This is where they remain, possessed and doomed to take medication to ease their alarming symptoms. But they can't be helped with pills because they have been taken over by a demonic force. That will be their permanent fate unless they are provided with an exorcism to free them.

However, not every soul that is being tormented by a demon needs an exorcism. It depends whether the torment is being caused by unwanted emotions and struggles, or whether they are just messing with the victim's mind. On the other hand, it may eventually succeed in possessing that person. This happens especially if the victim doesn't know what is happening or if they are a non-believer being oppressed by a demon that has attached itself to their soul and tries to control them.

If that happens, they will probably end up in a mental institution because they don't know what is happening and all the non-believers around them just assume that they've gone crazy. Or worse still, they end up losing all hope and join the homeless, drifting aimlessly on the streets. Some just turn to suicide.

It's difficult going through such a traumatic event and no-one is there to help you. This is why, after my experience with demons, I went on to write this book and share my experiences. I want to help those going through these same experiences, to help them understand that they are not alone, that someone believes in them and understands their pain. I want to be someone who can help by sharing my own experiences and spiritual knowledge.

Once I returned home from Melbourne, I still had to grapple with the ongoing horrors of my demonic oppression. As crazy as it may sound, many awful yet quite humorous events took place. I remember one night, I was in bed, trying to fall asleep. The room was incredibly quiet and out of nowhere the crucifix hanging on my wall flew across the room and almost hit me on the head. I got such a fright that I nearly fell out of bed. It was terrifying because I knew what it was, however, I tried to brush it off and tell myself that 'it couldn't hurt me'. Deep down I was terrified, because this could have been the beginning of an oppression right there and then.

A few weeks went by before, one day, I came home to find glass all over the floor. There was no-one home, but I noticed that a few photographs had fallen on the floor. They were pictures of me and my family. I picked them up and examined the damage and saw that the glass had cracked right across my face. It was trying hard, but I believe this demon wasn't as powerful as the ones I would encounter later on.

I didn't know what to do at this point, especially when it started escalating and getting worse. I could constantly hear knocking on my walls, growling in my ears, and constant scratching on the floors and walls. I even saw tall, dark shadows standing in the corner of my bedroom. As traumatic as these manifestations were, I grew somewhat accustomed to their presence, but I became so tired since I barely ever slept.

I remember one night, which was probably the last time I managed to sleep properly, I could feel and hear something at the base of my bed. I realised that I was asleep, but for the life of me, I could not wake myself up. I could feel something about the size of a dog jumping at the bottom of my bed where my feet were. I was so scared that I couldn't move or scream or even open my eyes. I thought my inability to move could have been sleep paralysis.

Eventually, taking all my energy and strength to do so, I finally managed to open my eyes. I was prepared for the worse, and expected to see a demon sitting on the end of my bed but whatever had been there was gone. The energy in the room became invisible, and my blanket was pulled off me. This experience left me sleeping like a child with my night light on. As a result, I can't and won't ever sleep in the dark again. These were just some of the awful demonic experiences I have had. I don't know why it didn't attach itself to me at that time, except that I wasn't as vulnerable then, or maybe that one wasn't convinced it could take over my soul. Many reasons can come into play.

Another night, the demonic oppression became extreme. Just like most other nights, I was relaxing at home when once again, I smelled an odour of rotten eggs and sulphur. Automatically, I knew what was going on. The awful energy in the room became so overwhelming that I felt dreadfully sick, tired and weak. I felt like I couldn't breathe and I felt like I was going to throw up at any moment. I was terribly afraid. I could sense just how badly it wanted me. They weaken you so that you will surrender, and then they can take control over your mind.

Luckily, I knew this, so I approached the local Bishop for help. I knew I was once again on the brink of possession. He did help me to some extent and I escaped being fully possessed, however, the demonic spirit latched itself to my soul and I experienced a demonic haunting for months. It was horrific. Just imagine being frightened every night, being tormented by ruthless spirits who want to destroy you and your soul. These experiences have left me permanently afraid and I honestly don't think anyone reading this could begin to understand that kind of fear unless they have experienced it themselves.

Having described what I've been through and what attracts a demon, I want to discuss how to recognise the signs that a demon is haunting you or your house.

My goal in writing this narrative is to tell my own story, but at the same time to guide others who believe that they might be in paranormal trouble. It can be difficult for troubled people to discern what is happening to them. It is a very real possibility that they are being targeted by demons, demonic infestation, and are at risk of possession. They could possibly think they're depressed but they may actually be going through a demonic infestation.

As I've said above, there's a difference between being possessed by a demon and being tormented by one. A demonic infestation generally leads to a possession, since that's the demon's main goal. To differentiate the two, this book will examine the signs of a demonic infestation and possession, so people can understand and find the appropriate help.

Demonic infestation. What is it? A demonic infestation is just like a ghost on a haunting, except that the goal is to scare their victim. They are a negative energy and will do things to hurt a person in order to make them weaker. Before we go into the signs of a demonic haunting, it is necessary to understand what attracts demons, in order to prevent it from ever happening.

It thought that demons may be attracted to people practicing dark magic or trying to summon a demon.

This is due to the fact that someone is actively seeking them out. No-one should never actively try and seek out a demon, since once a demon appears, it doesn't go away that easily. Additionally, if someone has negative energy due to stress, or anger or sleep deprivation, they may catch the attention of a demon because the negative energy will give them greater power. Although no-one really knows what prompts a demonic haunting people can take a few precautions. What I have learnt through my guides and my own demonic experiences enables me to summarise the most common causes.

One of the most obvious signs is strange noises. The sound of a demon is guttural, a harsh growling unlike anything an ordinary animal would produce. This may occur in specific locations, such as closets or hallways. Even strained words or disembodied voices can be heard over the shoulder, they could be asking questions, or threatening their victim in some way. Other sounds may also occur which include banging, stomping or scratching on walls. In some cases, people have reported hearing three unexplained knocks in a row... a number that is often repeated by demons as a mockery of the Holy Trinity. For that reason, 3am is their favourite hour to either begin their torment or to make what is already happening much worse.

Crazily enough, pets can be an indicator of demonic infestation. Many believe dogs, cats and other animals can actually see ghosts. When a dog starts barking at empty air, he may have witnessed a passing spirit. There are also those cases when the animal is terrified and even growling or hissing at an unseen force invisible to human eyes. A pet may begin acting aggressively for no apparent reason, and there are even some cases in which a pet has reportedly fallen ill during a demonic attack.

In 'True Tales of the Ouija Board', the author, Stephen Wagner, relates one such incident during which a group of girls were 'playing' with an Ouija board. All was well, until they contacted a spirit that unexpectedly mentioned their dogs. When they asked the spirit what it meant, it simply replied, "You'll see!"

Not long after that, the girls heard their dogs yelping wildly outside and later found a mysterious burn mark on one of them.

Jax, my Border Collie, would always sense whenever there was a negative spirit around. As dogs normally do when there's an intruder, they bark, shake and become agitated. Jax couldn't see it but because dogs have a heightened sense to spirits, he would always know when a presence was around, becoming anxious and afraid. The negative energy clearly had an effect on him. Jax disappeared around the lake one night and when he returned, he was vomiting and growling, and trying to bite us. He remained in this possessed state for about a week. I guess the demon thought if it couldn't get to me it will get my dog. But after that week had passed and Jax was more himself again, it was back hovering and messing with my thoughts and it wove itself into my soul again.

Seeing shadows can be another sign of a demonic haunting. Sightings of so-called shadow people may be an indication that a demon is present. In some cases, the shadows take humanoid forms but they've also appeared as animals or even as simple amorphous blobs that don't resemble anything at all. You may encounter brief glimpses in your peripheral vision, or they may appear as full shadows or black figures that glide and have a black hood with a white face. This is the form taken by the demon that oppressed my sister. It chose for me and my sister to see that under that hood was the most hideous looking soul you would ever see, with ghastly claws beyond measure.

Dreams are interesting things, but nightmares are also a sign of demonic haunting. They can tell us a lot about who we are, and what our subconscious minds are really thinking. They can also, perhaps, act as windows into a world just beyond our own. But that's not always a world we want to enter. Many have reported having strange and terrible dreams that accompany the unexplained activity in their homes during a haunting, particularly nightmares involving demons.

Demons don't take kindly to holy or religious symbols. They may attempt to get rid of crucifixes, Bibles, rosaries or other religious artifacts and will want to damage anything they view as a threat against their presence. For example, you may witness a hanging crucifix being knocked off the wall.

As I have already mentioned, odours are strong indicators of a demonic presence. One of the most common signs is a sudden, terrible, putrid smell. It is the odour of decomposition or sulphur-smelling rotting eggs, which is mimicking the scent of death. The sulphur smell is actually a reaction that a demon, or other negative entities, have to divinity. It is thought that this smell occurs when the demon is upset, or when the area they are inhabiting has been blessed or cleansed.

Another sign of demonic infestation is physical and mental disturbances where you have been scratched by an otherworldly force. A spiritual attack may have occurred when the victim experiences scratches, bite marks and other wounds without any ordinary explanation. They may happen anywhere on the body, or even on objects within the house with small, mysterious scratches that seem to defy all rationality. I have been attacked many times and have often woken to find huge scratch marks and dark bruises on me, always in a series of three.

In the case of a demon attack, like the aforementioned knocking sounds, three scratches or claw marks are said to serve as a mockery of the Holy Trinity. But scratches aren't the only sign related to spiritual attacks. A person may feel odd sensations, like he or she is being watched. Feelings of unease, or even outright nausea and other forms of illness have also been reported. The goal, it would seem, is to wear a person down to make their possession easier.

Demonic infestation is emotionally, spiritually and mentally scarring. It is important to realise that the demon's main goal is to break victims down enough in order to possess them and take control of their lives. They must try these tactics because they know that people are stronger than they are. If victims keep their composure and stay strong, there is nothing a demon can do. There are some things individuals can do to help themselves if ever they, or their home, has been infested by a demon.

Getting a demon to leave can be far more challenging than identifying one. The first defence is to actually ask them in a firm voice to leave, but many demons won't cooperate. If demanding that they leave doesn't work, that's where a respectable, experienced Bishop comes in. They can assess the home and the entity to determine what needs to be done. From a simple sage or incense cleansing, which typically just puts the intruder to sleep, to a full-blown ceremonial cleansing, such as an exorcism, it can be quite a process.

A cleansing or clearing can last anywhere from a few minutes to days. It all depends on how much of an attachment the demon has to the home and the people living within it. In my case, the demon had possessed half of my soul and I needed three exorcisms in total and I needed to maintain strong faith. Regardless of whether a person is religious or not, exorcisms can be extremely important, because they do work.

Keidi Pushi, an executive coach, healer and psychic shares that the key to getting spirits to leave, is to begin from a place of strength.

"I make sure I feel grounded and strong in myself. Standing in one area or walking around the house, I point a finger around the physical space that I am declaring to clear," she says. "I say my name and my right to claim the space as pure and as my own, and I ask the physical infrastructure of the house to hold only loving spirits."

Demonic oppression can be scary, it can be scarring, and it can be outright traumatic. It can harm people, their family and loved ones and even their pets. However, if someone is going through a demonic oppression, they will need to get help as soon as possible. This is because the sooner they recognise the nature of their oppressor, the sooner they can eliminate it before it potentially leads to possession. If someone unfortunately becomes possessed, death can result from even trying to cast out the demon.

Although death seldom occurs, it is a possibility that we don't ever want. Of utmost importance, is an emphasis on remaining strong. If a victim allows the demon to weaken them, it will eventually clamp its hold on their soul and possess them, holding on with immense tenacity.

CHAPTER FIVE

◆

The Exorcism

With my demonic oppression persisting for months at a time, my body became weaker and weaker from lack of sleep. I was angry, I was sad, I was in all kinds of emotional turmoil. I couldn't take being tormented any more. My spirit was growing weaker but I refused to give in, thinking only of love, happiness and prayer. I would speak to my demonic visitor mentally, telling it I was stronger, even though it certainly didn't feel like it much of the time. But I had to fight for myself and my children's safety.

This wavering gave the demon the perfect opportunity to take control over my soul and to possess my body. However, I held on with enough strength to keep control of part of my soul. This really helped with the exorcism as the demon was having trouble fully possessing me due to my inner strength and spiritual knowledge.

The exorcism began on the 20th March, 2014, in the living room of my home. Father Glenn arrived with Father Leon and a Christian lady name Gene, since a

Bishop can't perform an exorcism alone. Castings make demons very angry and you don't ever want to see how much fury they are capable of. It is truly more fearsome than fear itself. The Bishop and Father Leon put on their gowns and prepared their words to cast this demon out of me forever. Forever sounded like a dream to me, and a dream is exactly what it was for the demon later returned, or perhaps it was its friend that arrived since it is unusual for one to be cast out and then be able to return.

The exorcist gave me a candle to hold. He drew a cross on my forehead with holy water. He began to pray.

"In the name of the Father, the Son and the Holy Spirit."

Then he began to read his bible and as I wasn't yet possessed, I didn't have to be restrained. I only had part of my soul left under my control, but I was still fighting. At this point I knew exactly what was happening to me, therefore, I thanked God for my spiritual gift. Next, the powerful words that we prayed to save my soul began:

"In the name of the Father, the Son and the Holy Spirit. Amen.

Most glorious prince of the heavenly armies, Saint Michael the Archangel, defend us in our battle against principalities and powers, against the rulers of this world of darkness, against the spirits of wickedness in the high places.

Come to the assistance of men whom God has created in his likeness and whom he has redeemed at a great price from the tyranny of the devil. To you the Lord has entrusted the souls of the redeemed to be led into heaven. Pray therefore the God of Peace to crush

Satan beneath our feet, that he may no longer retain men captive and do injury to the church. Offer our prayers to the most high that without delay they may draw his mercy down upon us; take hold of the dragon, the old serpent, which is the devil and Satan, bind him and cast him into the bottomless pit so that he may no longer seduce the nations."

Afterwards came the actual exorcism, which read:

"In the name of Jesus Christ, our God and Lord, strengthened by the intercession of the immaculate Virgin Mary, Mother of God, of blessed Michael the archangel, of the blessed apostles Peter and Paul and all the saints, and powerful in the holy authority of our ministry.

We confidently undertake to repulse the attacks and deceits of the Devil. God arises; his enemies are scattered and those who hate him flee before him. As smoke is driven away, so are they driven; as wax melts before the fire, so the wicked perish at the presence of God.

Behold the cross of the Lord, flee bands of enemies. The lion of the Tribe of Juda, the offspring of David, hath conquered.

May the Lord defend upon us as great as our hope in thee.

We drive you from us, whoever you may be, unclean spirits, all Satanic powers, all infernal invaders, all wicked legions, assemblies and sects.

In the name and by the power of our Lord Jesus Christ, may you be snatched away and driven from the church of God and from the souls made to the image and likeness of God and redeemed by the precious blood of the divine lamb.

Most cunning serpent, you shall no more dare to deceive the human race, persecute the church, torment God's elect and sift them as wheat. The highest God commands you be with whom, in your great insolence, you still claim to be equal. God who wants all men to be saved and come to the knowledge of the truth.

God the Father commands you, God the Son commands you, God the Holy Ghost commands you. Christ, God's word made flesh, commands you. He who to save our race outdone through your envy humbled himself, becoming obedient even unto death.

He who has built his church on the firm rock and declared that the gates of hell shall not prevail against her, because he will dwell with her all days even to the end of the world.

The sacred sign of the cross commands you as do also the power of the mysteries of the Christian faith. Begone, Satan, inventor and master of all deceit, enemy of man's salvation. Give place to Christ in whom you have found none of your work; give place to the one, holy Christian church acquired by Christ at the price of his blood. Tremble and flee when we invoke the holy and terrible name of Jesus, this name to which causes hell to tremble. Holy, holy, holy, is the Lord, the God of Hosts. Lord hear my prayer, and let me cry unto thee, and with thy spirit let us pray.

God of heaven, God of Earth, God of angels, God of archangels, God of patriarchs, God of prophets, God of apostles, God of martyrs, God of virgins. God who has power to give life after death and rest after work.

For thou art the creator of all things, visible and invisible of whose reign there shall be no end. Deign, oh Lord, to grant us thy protection and to keep us safe and sound. We beseech thee through Jesus Christ our Lord. Amen."

Holy water was splashed round my home and on me and that was the end of the exorcism. Did it cast the demon out forever, like it was supposed to? How crazy does all of this sound so far? I thought the same until there was nothing, not a sound, not a scratch, not a peep from any soul after that. How could this be, I thought to myself, where did it go? Just like that... it was gone after some holy words had been read! It was finally gone, well at least for the next two years anyway. Had it just gone into hiding and wanted me to believe it was gone? Or did it lead its friends to me? Answers to those questions will be covered later on in this hard-to-believe story.

I have had a few experiences with exorcisms, and it is important to understand how and when they should be performed. So, for anybody who thinks they may need to, contact a Bishop and have an exorcism undertaken. Do it before it's too late.

When does someone need an exorcism? They will generally need an exorcism when they feel as though a demon has taken control over their body, or part of their body. What are the signs that someone has been possessed or oppressed?

One of the most obvious and common signs is when a person can't control themselves. Someone under the control of a demon cannot adequately control their bodily movements or functions, and may eat uncontrollably, become depressed and angry, or develop an obsession with sex. The evil spirit wants to experience all the things humans can do and it is able to speak through their lips or it can make them mute, whatever it desires.

However, there are multiple ways in which a demon can exercise control. Even if the person is not yet possessed and being oppressed, they will still experience overly emotional feelings, which is the main indication that I experienced. They might feel incredibly angry, sad, guilty or any other negative emotion, for no particular reason. Maybe they have found themselves somewhere without thinking about going there or remembering going there. This could be a sign that a demon has taken control of their movements.

Another sign, that can be hard to decipher is taking on another personality. Maybe their nature, suddenly changes without an obvious cause. Perhaps they used to be happy, loud and extroverted and then suddenly became introverted and sad. This change in personality can be a sign. Along with that, they could experience a 'split-personality'. However, be aware that this can also be a mental illness as well, so it's important to understand that there is a difference. Someone could feel as though someone else is living within them, because that's what a possession actually is. This occupation of the victim's personality will be an evil spirit, and it could drive them to do evil, horrific deeds and dwell on all things negative.

Episodes of blacking out is another important sign that someone may be possessed. Perhaps they don't remember doing things, that others have told them they've done. Maybe they can't remember specific things that might have happened throughout the day. They might find themselves wet and wrapped in a bath towel, but don't remember going for a shower. This could be the demon taking control over the body for a short period of time. If the victim is not prone to mental illness and has never suffered any form of it, then pay extra attention.

Being so very vulnerable, the mentally ill are well known to be open to evil. They are easier targets, because they often rely on medications to stabilise their emotions and behaviour. However, even the mentally ill can tell the difference between their actual illness or a demonic haunting but being mental patients, generally no-one wants to believe them. If a mentally ill person is a spiritual non-believer then unfortunately, they will never be rescued and their soul will be owned by the demon permanently. Even after death there is little chance of that soul being saved.

Many people who are possessed have the ability to speak in another language. Usually the language is known as 'speaking in tongues' or 'tongues', but it could be Latin or any other language. A common language spoken by demons is Arabic.

Self-harm is another sign that one may be possessed. A demon loves to feed off pain and death which is why they cause people to harm themselves, such as by cutting themselves. This is because they want to destroy the person they possess. This happened to my sister, which is what made me recognise her oppression. That and the fact that she had actually seen a demon. I know that through my intervention for her, the demon left my sister and chose to attack me because helping others to recognise them makes them really angry.

These are just a few of the common signs, however, is not a precise thing and different people may have different indications. This is why it's important to contact a church if someone believes that they are possessed or being oppressed. Getting knowledge and support from an expert will help victims decipher what is going on and take decisive action.

CHAPTER SIX

◆

Fresh Start

Two years of peaceful daily routines passed without a peep from the evil spirit world. I had forced myself to move beyond it, even though it took a lot of courage and bravery. I was eventually strong and independent enough to go about my everyday life without fear.

However, for quite some time the ordeal left me afraid to be alone in my home, whether it be day or night. Thank goodness I got there with the help of my new found faith after such a horrific experience. I had no other means of protecting myself, but I was very glad I had found my faith and found it amazing how a higher power could be capable of saving me. I will be elaborating further at the end of the book on the stress disorder that these events instilled in me and I will give advice on how to recover.

My son was entering high school in the new year and I couldn't believe he was now a teenager. He was, and is, such a blessed and beautiful soul, although the older he got, the more I wanted another child. I swore to myself that one was plenty and I would never have another child. But while deciding whether or not I really did want another child, I fell pregnant! I was a little shocked, but tremendously happy and excited at the same time. Kieran didn't know how to take the news at first but he gradually became more and more enthusiastic. We started preparing for the baby's arrival since I knew nine months would go by very quickly. What I didn't know was that it would end up being just seven months.

At the 21-week scan, I was able to find out the sex of the baby. I had been hoping and praying for a daughter and I had made myself believe that it was going to be a baby girl. I had even picked out the name, Everly Eden Rose. As the day came closer, I couldn't wait to hear what the baby was, although was almost certain it was going to be a girl. The day of my scan arrived, and the ultrasound began, but to my surprise the baby was a boy!

However, he was healthy and normal. I have to say that I was slightly disappointed, but still happy all the same, since I was having a healthy child. Problem was, I didn't have any boy's names planned out as I just wasn't planning on having a boy, but there he was, inside my belly and growing fast. I did once see a vision of a girl and later on Phoebe had a girl, whom she named Evie Rose, so perhaps that was the girl that I saw in my vision.

I had always loved the name Spencer, whether it was for a boy or girl so Kieran and I agreed that Spencer was what his first name should be. For his middle name he would be named after Kieran's best friend, who died in a car accident when they were younger. The friend's name was Keegan. Personally, I was glad I had thought of a name quite soon after he came along so, Spencer Keegan it was.

One night I developed a severe pain beneath my ribs, on my back, and I asked Kieran to rub it, thinking maybe it was because my bra was too tight. However, it didn't relieve the pain. I tolerated the pain for a further five nights until I couldn't stand it anymore. By then I can honestly say I felt like I was dying and I asked Kieran to take me immediately to the hospital. It turned out that I was indeed dying and if I had let the situation go for another week, I would not be writing this narrative today.

We arrived at Wangaratta Base Hospital and went into the emergency ward, where I had to wait a little while before being seen by a doctor. I was in pure agony, wishing they would hurry up. Finally, a nurse came and took me to a room to check my vital signs and found that my blood pressure was extremely high. I was taken into another room to be seen by a doctor and have a blood test. In the meantime, I was given injections of morphine and oxycodone to diminish the pain, but unfortunately neither of those worked too well. Then I began to throw up heavily for a while. It was just terrible. The doctor came back in and explained to me that I had HELLP (haemolysis, elevated liver enzymes, low platelet count) syndrome. Only one in twenty thousand women will develop this affliction, which is due to their partner's DNA during pregnancy. I was unlucky enough to be one of them.

With HELLP, your liver begins to shut down and your blood platelets decline at a rapid rate, causing you to bleed internally. Therefore, the pregnancy had to be terminated as soon as possible if both mother and child were going to survive. Wangaratta did not arrange an emergency Caesarean section for me, even though that was what had to be done. They fed me tablets to keep Spencer in and injected me with steroids to assist his growth since his weight was only around four pounds. They felt that he might not survive past 29 weeks. I was just seven months pregnant and my baby had to be delivered. I was terrified, since at first I didn't understand the severity of HELLP. I soon learnt that this disorder had the potential to be fatal. It seemed that although being inflicted by HELLP, that was exactly what I needed at the moment.

Women with platelet levels of 40 did not usually survive, and nor did their babies. Alarmingly, my platelet levels continued to drop to 19 and I was starting to bleed internally. Blood was running freely through my body. I started to spit out clots and large amounts of dark red blood. Thankfully, I was not fully conscious due to the morphine.

Wangaratta hospital finally organised for me to be transported to Wodonga Hospital since they didn't have enough platelets for the transfusion that I required. My platelet levels had dropped from four hundred to 19 and I was bleeding significantly from my gums, and had begun bleeding internally. Once I arrived, they sent me for an MRI scan, which seemed unnecessary because they were already aware that I had HELLP syndrome.

I desperately needed a transfusion so I would be strong enough to go through with an emergency Caesarean. My pain level was unbearable and I was delusional from all the medication. On top of that, I was frightened half to death that I was going to die and possibly my baby would, too. Finally, a doctor announced that they didn't have enough platelets to give me here, either, so I had to be flown by helicopter to

Melbourne's Mercy Hospital where they could treat me appropriately. It was upsetting that they had wasted so much precious time which could possibly have resulted in me or my baby's death. I don't remember much of the short helicopter trip down to Melbourne, only that it was a stormy night and it was very dangerous for my mum, Kieran and Cody to be travelling by road to meet me in Melbourne.

Once I arrived, I had two platelet transfusions and was rushed in for an emergency Caesarean. I was given another blood transfusion and taken to the intensive care unit for recovery, while Spencer was taken to the special care for babies room, where he would remain for nine nights.

I needed intensive care to recover from the syndrome. After those nine torturous days came to an end, it was finally time for me to return home. I left the hospital covered in bruises from all the daily needles I had to have and was still in pain from the incision. Kieran and I got into the car to begin our trip back to Beechworth. Spencer was flown via helicopter to the Wodonga Nursery to be cared for until he gained some more weight and became a little more independent, which turned into a further 21 days. Meanwhile, I was still in so much pain trying to recover from the C-section and liver failure, and I was very weak for a while after my release from hospital.

We drove in and out of Wodonga to visit Spencer twice a day, primarily for me to breast-feed him. I couldn't bear leaving my newborn every day, it was so hard for me. This little boy we had created was so strong and smart, growing quickly and breastfeeding well for a premature baby. I was so proud of him. He stayed in the nursery until I was finally able to bring him home, where he belonged. Spencer was such a beautiful baby. He did wake quite a lot throughout the night during the first four months, and of course that was very tiring for me. However, I couldn't have been any happier or prouder of him, proud to have another beautiful son, and happy for us to both be alive.

As time went on, Spencer grew fast and I felt it was time to organise his christening since he was now nine months old. Not being religious, Kieran of course did not approve of this though it was important to me, so he accepted it. My religious dedication may seem over-zealous but remember, it was through Jesus that I had been able to escape my dreadful demonic affliction and I didn't quickly forget that.

So, whereas it may viewed as some sort of fervent dedication, I wanted him to be a part of a Christian community and most of all, I wanted him protected as one of God's children. I realise that this story will not be for everyone. I understand that and it is okay with me. I believe everyone is entitled to their own beliefs and I want to share my own experiences in the hope of reaching out to some people that have experienced the same struggles. Without my awful experience I would never have believed such a thing existed and I definitely didn't think it could happen to me. But it did.

Before Spencer turned one, we felt we needed more space, both indoors and outdoors, for the kids. So, we decided to move down the street into a four-bedroom house on one acre of land by the creek. Yes, a creek! That did initially put me off for a little while, since I knew creeks can be where evil lurks at night. However, I bravely pushed through this thought and we began moving our belongings into the new house. It was such a beautiful spot that I was so glad we found the place. It was a beautiful home, and it came with plenty of space for the kids to roam and enjoy.

We moved into our new home in January and then on the 22nd of April, Spencer turned one. My little chicken, as I called him then which is somewhat an accurate description of him, was already turning one! We bought him a two-kilogram, pear and date cake. It was so delicious and he loved it just as much as we did. The party we threw for him was nothing fancy, just a couple of friends and family to celebrate his big day. It felt crazy to me how fast time was marching on since I could still remember the day when he was born and how scared I was for both our lives. I felt so lucky to have both of my beautiful boys so strong and healthy.

Life sped by and I had almost begun to feel completely safe and free again, ready to forget the troubles that had entered my life and had tried to harm me. Then one night, Cody was in his room when his guitar started to strum all by itself and his jacket moved across the floor. He immediately came and told me about it. I froze in fear, and thought to myself, "Oh God, no, not again. Why us?"

We tried to ignore that incident even though seeing was believing, and we went on with our everyday lives.

About a week later, I woke up for no reason at all just past 2am, to smell that horrible stench of sulphur once again. I panicked and moved over to lie closer to Kieran. I attempted to explain to him, but of course he shut me down as soon as I began to mention a word of it. This made me feel so alone that I didn't know what to do. I was so scared and worried. I didn't want to go through it all again. The very next day I called Father Thomas and arranged for him to come and bless my house again. He agreed and came over straightaway to bless our home, but I still didn't feel safe.

My intuition served me right once again, because one night I was lying in bed with the light on, speaking to my dad on the phone with Spencer lying beside me on the floor. Then all of a sudden, he screamed.

"Mum!"

He was terrified. He ran up to me making these dreadful growling sounds and weird head movements, trying to emulate what he had just seen. I had never seen him so frightened in my life, but I knew what he had seen. The following day, I called Father Thomas again and I told him that this has to stop. We needed help. Why was this happening to us? Was it the same demon? Has it followed me? Or has it been here this whole time, playing hide and seek?

So many questions ran through my traumatised mind. Most importantly, I wanted my family to be safe. I wanted this evil demon gone and out of my happy home. Father Thomas called Bishop John from Wangaratta Anglican Church to see if he could be of any assistance in providing yet another exorcism.

I felt completely and utterly shattered. My life had been so good up to this point. I had been moving on. I had my wonderful family and my beautiful house. When we had to call for another exorcism, my heart sank. I was confused, angry and sad. I wanted the torment to stop. Yet, it carried on and on... and on.

◆

CHAPTER SEVEN

Here We Go Again

One day, I was in the shower singing away to Madonna, when my glass shower door banged aggressively.

I thought to myself, "What have I done to deserve this constant torture? Okay, Jesus, if you saved me before and cast it away, why is it back to haunt me?"

I was terribly confused and was reliving all that fear that I thought had been put to rest. Yet here we go again. I was having to go through yet another blessing by a Bishop. I was very angry.

Bishop John, Father Thomas, and Gene all turned up at my house once again, to perform their prayer to cast out the demon in Jesus' name. At this point I was starting to feel very uncertain about the blessing. I started to wonder if the demon had actually been eliminated the first time around. I didn't understand how or why it had followed me here to my new home and was continuing to try to destroy me. The Bishop did his work, while my son and I prayed that hopefully that would be it, this time, that it would now be banished for good. What else could we do?

A year later, I came across another demon, although this time it didn't attach itself to me. It only tormented me from a distance. So, I just continued to pray each night and tried to remain strong and positive. I needed to fight this beast and not allow myself to be vulnerable at any cost. I wasn't going to let this thing possess me or oppress me again, because it almost won the first time. It wasn't going to even come close to taking over my soul. I simply wasn't going to allow it. I refused to submit. The first time, I was extremely vulnerable, afraid and weak, which is why I believe this second attempt at possession was happening to me. They saw an easy mark.

My main concerns of course were for my boys. I was afraid that it would also try to oppress them. Spencer, I think, had experienced spiritual contacts a few times. He had seen many things that were quite strange and now that he could talk, what he was able to explain became much clearer to me. Because Spencer was such a young child, he was more open to these things. His mind hadn't been closed off to the spiritual realm. While children's minds are constantly developing as they grow, they are very vulnerable. They don't have any limitations of life and belief systems already fully instilled. They haven't learnt that 'ghosts don't exist', so that limitation isn't there. We stayed resident in that house for a further three years and three more incidents occurred.

I ended up calling a man named Father Allan, who came out to bless the home since Father Thomas was no longer sure how to help me. Being a fairly new priest, he had never actually experienced this phenomenon before.

However, the other new Bishops that helped me had dealt with quite a few cases, which was very reassuring. After what I had told them, they revealed that they had experienced similar situations with other people who had needed to be exorcised, of which only two had actually been possessed.

Some of those cases were worse off than I. However, any sort of torment, oppression or possession is such an ordeal, one's soul can never fully recover. I believe that the demon tries to take over and push your soul out of your body. The soul resists, but a piece of it may leave the body in an attempt to escape the ordeal and this piece is very hard to retrieve. It was incredibly traumatic trying to save myself from this situation.

That was the last exorcism I have experienced, to date. We have recently moved into another, more modern house which is not near a swamp or creek. I haven't as yet felt the presence of a demon, entity, spirit or ghost in my house. I do still have doubts about whether the demons are actually gone, or if they are just hiding until I feel completely safe. Perhaps they are trying to alter my thoughts and decisions subconsciously from a distance, creating anger and resentment that might lead me to sinful temptations and make me vulnerable again.

What is it that actually attracts a demon? For example, heavy metal music may attract demons, since this type of music is hostile, often violent and can create anger within a person. The altered state of mind attracts demons because they exploit suffering from internal anger. This gives them an opportunity to target certain people, and they thrive off it.

Insecurity and self-doubt are also contributing factors that allow one to be open to oppression, torment or possession. Low self-esteem makes the human spirit incredibly vulnerable, as the energy they emit is extremely low. Negative entities thrive off low energy and are therefore attracted. They won't hesitate to attach themselves to these vulnerable people. Some people may have more than one demon oppressing them at a time and can go a lifetime without knowing what is happening. If a demon detects a human soul free of possession, they dive on that soul to make the most of that person before another demon can finds its way there.

Using medications or prescribed drugs, and non-prescribed drugs, are another aspect of behaviour that can attract a demon. I have stressed these things earlier, but I want to elaborate a little further as to what happens when you consume these substances. The brain is altered by using drugs, even if it benefits you. However, the altered brain is also a gateway for a demon to enter, because we are temporarily in a weak state of mind and vulnerable. This creates a sort of crack in your chakra system, or your spirit. This can then become the portal for a demon to penetrate.

Then comes the concept of sin, which may sound incredibly crazy, although perhaps all of this does. To sin is to bring shame down upon yourself, according to God. It is not how he wants people to live their lives. He wants us to walk with him in life and live as he would. This of course means no lying, no infidelities, no deceit, no stealing or anything that goes against his preachings. However, as we are God's children and should never sin, demons love it when we go against God. They use sin as ammunition as well as a means for making their way into our souls. So, sin is what demons actually want us to do. Then they don't need to intervene to destroy us because we are already doing that to ourselves. They can simply just sit back and watch until we are weak and vulnerable enough for them to possess us.

In some cases, a severely depressed person who may feel suicidal, will receive encouragement from a demon. The invader pushes that destructive feeling upon them more and more, until they follow through with it. Then the demon's work is done because the person will have destroyed themselves and it can move on to the next vulnerable soul.

THE APPEARANCE OF DEMONS?

It is important to understand that spirits that have once lived as humans do not have the spiritual energy to move things. These spirits will come to people through their dreams, via an animal or even perhaps through a song. But, if things begin to violently move or bang, or the blanket gets pulled off at night, it is an entity that has never lived. These are the only ones with the power to do such things. For non-believers, if similar things begin happening, they may feel like they're going crazy but they know they're not. Or, maybe there's a bad smell or they see something move without a logical explanation, then religious or not, they should reach out and seek help from a Bishop.

Demons can appear in whatever form they want their victims to see them as. These manipulating and deceitful beings can portray themselves in multiple forms. Sometimes they like to act as innocent, loving spirits that might need help, or perhaps they act as a loved one that has passed on. They do this in order to deceive people, hoping to gain trust so their victims will open up their life to them. Just because a spirit seems charming, we must remind ourselves that it may very well be an evil spirit looking to gain leverage.

Demons are evil, ugly, black souled spirits. Their true form is usually black hooded, gliding along with just a white face and long claws, which they use to scratch victims in their sleep. They are evil and scary phenomena that work to inflict fear into our lives, and their horrible appearance goes a long way to achieve that. Demons are also very powerful because they have never walked the earth. Their spiritual strength is phenomenal, and they even have the ability to throw a person or an object right across a room.

I don't wish my experiences with such nasty beings upon anybody else, but it's important to note that prior to these awful experiences, I was not very religious. However, I have found that the stronger my Christian belief is and the more I pray and seek Jesus, the safer I have been. I am sure this must sound silly to some people, but I strongly feel my story needs to be told and you can take whatever you wish from it. If sharing my spiritual insights with others makes me sound crazy, I don't care... it's worthwhile. If I succeed in helping even one other tormented person, then I have achieved what I set out to do.

CHAPTER EIGHT

◆

The Good Ones

It can be quite disheartening and frightening to read the capabilities of demons, especially if you're experiencing a spirit in your home. However, not all spirits are bad. Some can be positive and are important in our lives.

GOOD SPIRITS

In this next section I will identify the different kinds of good or positive spirits that come in and out of our lives. Some remain with a person all the time simply to look out for them, while others may try to get a particular message across and when that's accomplished, they leave. These ones are more likely to be angels. So, is there any magic to all of this, and what about miracles?

Human bodies are just handy vehicles that our souls inhabit temporarily, but where do we go once we are done with our human form? Some people think nowhere... you just die, and it all goes to black, it's 'lights out!' Others, like me, know it's not like that at all. But, how can I possibly know this is true?

Well... as I grew older, my spiritual connection with my own spiritual guides became stronger and I was able to connect with them through my mind. Also, when I was sleeping, spirits would pass on messages to me. Whether we realise it or not, spiritual guides are an important aspect of our lives, since they're always there to help us in some way or other. Now, there's not just my guides, but my grandad is also there beside me, guiding me through my life. Sometimes he just visits to let me know he is there, while other times he has passed important messages across to me.

Although I only hear what they are telling me when I tune in, and I don't know how to communicate in return, my spirit guides speak to me and fill my mind with things I need to know. I seem to possess great intuition and have a gift to understand a person without knowing them. I can tell people all about themselves without them saying a word, the very first time I meet them. This is an important part of my psychic capabilities, which I will expand upon later.

So, although it is clear to me that the afterlife exists, seeing is believing, hearing is believing, and feeling is believing. Once we pass away, we rise above our body and continue to float up until we join the spirit world. Then we are approached by three angels known as Archangel Michael, Archangel Gabriel and Archangel Raphael. They go through your life along with you, starting at your birth. This process is the soul being judged and also forgiven. It's sort of a slide show of your life to recall later in heaven, and if you have made too many mistakes, perhaps you will eventually get an opportunity to go back and rectify those in a new human form.

One spirit that I had seen in my mind is Jesus. He may be present at the time of your passing, although perhaps not for everybody and maybe it's only the religious who see him. However, once the initial meeting with the angels is complete, you walk with them deeper into the spirit world. I have had visions of doing this when performing readings for people who have lost loved ones.

This spiritual place looked so beautiful, with the sun shining and giant flowers everywhere. All of the souls that had made it to old age before passing had regained their youth. The wrinkles that were once there had been completely wiped away. This place is like magic. Words are insufficient to describe the beauty and love that abounds in heaven. Knowing that this beautiful place is where spirits go after life, made the acceptance of death much easier for me to comprehend.

What is hard for all of us here in the living dimension is that we can't see our loved ones, and some can't even feel them anymore. Unless you are blessed with a psychic ability, and even if not, if you tune yourself in enough and really want to find them... you will. We all receive messages from heaven, you just have to pay attention and understand beyond what you can physically see and feel.

The spirits that have reached their celestial home are in a wonderful place, they are at peace and full of joy and happiness. They continue to be by our side and support us through the rest of our life's journey. So, don't fear they are forever lost, they are not gone and we will see them again, just in a different form. Hopefully, I can impart to others some reassurance and hope so they can find some comfort.

"I watch you of a morning as the sun shines on you as you sleep. I see you view my photo and it hurts me when you weep. I know that you can't hear me but I listen to all of your dreams. You think you will never see me again but it's not all as it seems. Because up here we do magic and miracles are for me. I'll soon be close by you but at first you still won't be able to see, as I will take another form different from the one before. Then I'll be able to hold you and there's nothing I want more. You won't recognise me at first but soon you will get to know, you will remember all the little things that made you love me so."

Although we are all able to enter this spirit world known as heaven, some souls get attached to things in the living world, like a particular location, perhaps a house. However, they are not really in the living world anymore, they are now on a different plane. I wouldn't like sharing my home with a spirit who is reluctant to move on and some of us may feel or see a ghostly presence, but don't be afraid since they are not malicious. They will leave in their own time. And if not... you are safe anyway. Some spirits like to be seen, so they will reveal themselves to get attention, not to hurt anyone but just to let us know that they are there. While others can be heard or felt, wandering about the place.

It is also possible to encounter a child soul, who loves to play since they are still young. They remain young forever and are generally attracted to living children, but sometimes they can cause a fright without meaning to. Children's minds are spiritually open to this other world and I have quite often heard of children speaking to someone that adults can't see. If this ever happens to you, don't worry unless the signs of evil are present. Examples of evil are things moving around the home, a bad smell or if your child starts speaking nonsense in violent ways, shows aggression, stays awake all night or grows a huge appetite.

There are seven archangels that guide us through life, Michael, Gabriel, Raphael, Ariel, Zadkiel, Chamuel and Uriel. These angels all have different roles to play, but in one way or another, they all help us to bring happiness, love and peace into our lives.

The name Archangel Michael means "he who is like God." He is the leader of the archangels and is known for his war against Satan. Michael is there for guidance in the areas of career and ambitions. You can pray to Archangel Michael for protection for your home, family and loved ones. He will guide you in order to grow spiritually and emotionally. He will help give you courage to make the changes that are necessary for success.

Archangel Gabriel is the second highest ranking after Michael. His name means "strength" and he is known to be a messenger and communicator. He helps in areas of communication as well as in creative expression. If you possess psychic abilities, it is important to ask Archangel Gabriel for clear messages. He also brings strength to those conceiving a child.

Archangel Raphael brings healing to living beings, whether it's physical, emotional or spiritual and he represents "the healing power of God." If you are involved in healing work, you can pray to Archangel Raphael for assistance. You can also call to him for assistance with travel plans, helping to ensure that you and your belongings are protected and most importantly, safe.

Archangel Ariel protects and heals living things in nature. His name means "Lion of God." He protects animals, fish, birds, plants and the elements. You can call to Archangel Ariel for the healing of your pets, and when you need guidance for grounding and connection.

Archangel Zadkiel is the archangel of mercy. His name means "Righteousness of God." Call on Zadkiel when you have difficulty forgiving yourself or others. He can also help you bring kindness back into your life and help you move forward. He is a healer of the mind and can guide you to getting out from being stuck in emotional baggage and failures. Zadkiel will help you to see things clearly and give you strength to let go of toxic relationships. He will also guide you to grow spiritually.

Archangel Chamuel is the angel of harmonious and loving relationships. His name means "he who sees" and he is kind and empathic. He can help you to develop sincere and deep feelings within. You can call to Archangel Chamuel when you're in need of help with your relationships and partnerships. He can help to teach you how to love yourself and give you strength to end any harmful relationships.

Archangel Uriel takes you out of darkness into divine light. His name means "God is Light." You can call to Archangel Uriel when you're confused about what God's path is for you. If you are stuck in life, and looking for inspiration, pray to Uriel for guidance. He will help you transform your life and yourself into something better. Uriel will also help you in love and protect you from negative energies.

While Archangels guide us through life, they're not the only ones. We also have our own spirits who guide us throughout our lives. These spirit guides are divine beings that get assigned to us before we are born. They help us fulfill the spiritual contract we have set before our incarnation. What is known as your higher self, helps us choose these guides that help us throughout our life.

But just who are these guides? While some guides stay with you through your entire life, others come in now and then when you need help, perhaps for a specific aspect of your life. These guides have a variety of consciousnesses. Some might be highly ascended, while others are your average spirit who has deep wisdom within a certain area. They may appear as having female or male energy, but either way they're just divine energy. These angel spirits may have had a human life-form in the past, while others have never lived a human experience. They may be guiding you alone, or they may have a group of other souls as well. They also could be a deceased relative, however this is unlikely. Your spirit guide tunes into your energy and directs you to fulfill your life's purpose, while deceased relatives usually appear for comfort and to say hello.

How do they guide us? Spirit guides can see what is happening in our lives. They contact us in a variety of ways when it's time for them to intervene, by sending signs. They create synchronicities in our life, or what you could call a coincidence, to help us become aware of something important. You should always pay attention when something like that happens, because I believe there is no such thing as a coincidence and everything in my view is fate. Our spirit guides love to put signs in our path, whether it's numbers, a particular song on the radio or an animal that returns to your property each day for a period of time.

Spirit guides also communicate with us, through our intuition, which we often refer to as 'our gut feeling.' Following your gut feeling is often a good thing. Have you ever met someone new and something seemed just a little bit off about them? That is your intuition working for you. Intuition is seldom wrong, so go with it unless you suffer from severe anxiety, in which case it might just be paranoia you are experiencing.

Another way your spirit guides will communicate with you, is through intuitive insight. This is flashes of intuition which might sound like a voice, telling you to slow down, realising ahead of time that you very well could have been in a car accident. These are random thoughts that seem to come out of thin air. These thoughts are divine and contain important information. However, many tune out of their intuition by second-guessing these feelings of awareness.

Spirit guides also send people into our lives by arranging with someone else's spirit guides, for a meeting between you and someone else. Have you ever thought about someone and then saw them walking around in the shop? This is your spirit guide trying to create a meeting between the two of you. Sometimes, we are guided to someone to hear divine words from them. Sometimes people may tell you powerful things, that were divinely guided to make you realise something you should have already seen. Or maybe it's your soulmate, a soulmate however can be an animal or human.

Another way spirit guides can help you, is by re-arranging things. Perhaps you're running late and can't find your keys, only to notice you get an important call from someone. You would never have received the call if you had found your keys and left on time. This is hard to believe and seldom happens since we have our own free will, but could it have been your spirit guides that misplaced the keys? Sometimes you just need to surrender during frustrating moments, because it could be a blessing in disguise.

Spirit guides are divine and beautiful. They fill your life with blessings and abundance and try to help you through life. They also remind you that you are not alone on your journey, so please take a little time to hear them and thank them, and accept that they are there.

Another form of a spirit guide is what's known as an animal guide or animal totem. A spirit animal is a teacher or messenger that comes in the form of an animal, which has a personal relationship to an individual. In Shamanic traditions, it was believed that every animal had a certain energy attached to it, and one could call on that animal spirit to help guide and protect them. For example, someone can call on the butterfly when they're in need of transformation in their life.

When you see a certain animal everywhere you look, whether it's real or not, chances are there is a message for you. It's important to understand that you don't pick your spirit guides, but that they pick you. These animals can come to you in your dreams, meditations or in real-life and are a reflection of your deepest self, which is important to acknowledge. This type of guide comes to deliver a specific message or warning and leaves once it has been understood.

There are eight main animal guides in your life; the shadow, journey, life, land, water, bird, reptile and insect guides. However, it's important to understand the meaning behind any animal in your life.

The first and main animal guide is the shadow guide. This animal represents your shadow self or the biggest fear that you need to overcome in order to progress in your life. It helps to show us the unhealed aspects of ourselves that require attention. This is a powerful guide and changes throughout your life. For example, you could see a crow, which represents death, and calls for you to let go of your fear of death.

The second main animal guide is the journey guide. This animal might show up when you're at a crossroads in your life, or in need of making an important decision. This guide will lead you through a particular journey and represents the challenges and rewards. It will help you to choose the best path and guide you when you are lost.

Next, we have the life animal guide. This animal represents your inner spiritual self. This guide is always with you, whether you notice it or not. It's similar to an archangel, who is always looking out for and protecting you.

In Shamanic religion, they will call on the spirit of a specific animal, bird, fish, reptile or insect. Each of these groups have a special meaning, although each animal has its own individual meaning.

The land animals are associated with being grounded, as well as mental and psychical stability. They are filled with high intuition and awareness. Call on a land animal guide when you're in need of grounding and stability.

The water animal guide represents freedom, cleansing and clarity. They are a symbol of the universal unconsciousness that passes messages to us through dreams and the subconscious mind. Call on the water animal guide when you're in need of clarity or purification.

The bird guides symbolise new transitions in life, guiding us in matters of higher wisdom. They have excellent foresight and intuition. Call on a bird animal guide when you're in need of 'seeing the bigger picture.'

Reptile guides are a symbol of adaptation. They are highly independent and strong. They remind us that every situation can help us to grow. Call on a reptile guide when you're in need of growth and adaptation.

Finally, there is the insect guide, which brings the gift of patience, non-attachment and tenacity. They are transformational, just like the reptiles. Call on insect guides when you're in need of patience or personal transformation.

But how can you find your spirit animal guides? This is a sacred practice, and it requires long periods of focus. It won't happen in a day. It is advised to meditate or visualise your animal totem. However, before that, it's suggested that you should think and focus on it throughout the day.

Repeat to yourself, "I'm ready to find my spirit guides."

Additionally, we have free will, so it's important to ask your spirit guides to reveal themselves to you. Remember that they choose us, we don't choose them, so pay attention to what animals show up in your life. An animal that is continuously showing up in your life, may very well be one of your animal spirit guides.

Another form of spirit guide are ancestral guides. Ancestral guides are entities that have some kind of blood connection to us due to our shared lineage. An ancestral guide could be a recently deceased member of your family (mother, father, aunt, grandfather), or a long-departed relative that you could never have met in your lifetime. Having done shamanic journeying in the past, I connected with what I consider to be my ancestors. To me, they appeared as shadowy beings that felt distinctly familiar. They taught me that although I sometimes felt alone and isolated in my current family, I was part of something vastly larger. The messages that our ancestors bring can be beautiful and life-changing.

Now that you have knowledge of the different kinds of good spirits and guides, you will also want to know how to contact them. However, as discussed later in the 'séance' chapter, it can be very dangerous to do so, because this practice can easily attract spirits of all kinds into your life; including demons. Nonetheless, I'll give you guidance on how to contact them. Some methods can be dangerous while other ways, are much less problematic.

'Scrying' is one way to contact your spirit guides. However, this can be dangerous since it can create a portal for any spirits to come into your life, so it is important to be cautious.

Scrying is the ancient divinatory practice of gazing into a reflective surface, such as water, mirrors, or crystal balls to receive esoteric information. From a psychological perspective, scrying helps you get in touch with your unconscious mind and the important guidance, which may be locked away within it.

Scrying is something that must be practiced consistently, since it is not easy. However, it is worth committing to if you are a visually based person (i.e. one who receives insight through pictures, also known as clairvoyance). In order to connect with your spirit guide via scrying, set an intention to 'see' your guide. You may like to repeat a mantra or prayer to communicate with the guide that you wish to meet them.

Dream work is another method you may employ to contact your spirit guides, which is luckily much safer than scrying. Just before going to bed, set the intention to see, meet or speak with your spirit guide within your dreams. Continue this practice for two weeks and see what happens. When you wake up, note any strange figures or unusual patterns that emerge from your dream. The goal is to find repetition in what messages or dream beings keep appearing.

Sometimes our spirit guides don't directly reveal themselves, but instead symbolically reveal who they are to us. Take note of symbols that keep emerging and write in your journal about them. What do they mean? Once you have a strong inkling of who or what your guide is, you should thank them. Continue to ask for guidance and for their appearance in your dreams before going to bed. Learning how to lucid dream is also a powerful way to contact your spirit guides.

Meditation is not only a good way to relieve stress, but a way you can hear your spirit guides. One of the best ways to contact your spirit guides is by silencing your mind through practices such as meditation or mindfulness.

Here is one simple practice: Sit or lie down in a quiet place that is undisturbed by other people. Focus on your back or thighs as they come in contact with the ground. Notice the rising and falling of your chest. Listen to the sounds around you. Focus on being present in the 'now'. If you have raging thoughts, jump up and down for a little bit (to expel the frantic energy from your body), then resume your meditation.

Let your thoughts become like a stream. Sit down and watch that stream as a silent observer. Don't try to fight these thoughts, just let them flow. When you feel ready, ask to hear the name or see the face of your spirit guide. You might need to wait for a while, so be patient. Let go of expectations (they will block what you are about to receive). Write about your experiences afterward, jot down notes and feelings. If you struggle with this practice, don't worry. Most people do. Just practice it for 10 minutes a day and see what happens.

Bibliomancy is another great practice, which is the practice of seeking spiritual insight by opening a book at a random place. This form of divination was popular in the middle ages, but it continues to be an interesting way of gaining guidance.

Here is how to use bibliomancy to connect with your spirit guides: Go to your personal library or collection of books, or alternatively, you can go to a local library. Stand in front of the books and close your eyes. Ask to be drawn to a specific book that will help reveal your spirit guide. I encourage closing your eyes as you do this so that you aren't influenced by bias. Let your inner feelings guide you. When you feel a pull, run your hands over the bookcase or pile of books. Pick the book you feel most drawn to, but remember to keep your eyes shut! Then, either open the book at random and quickly look at the page or wait for a page number to pop into your mind, then read that page in the book you have randomly selected.

Sometimes 'bibliomancy' works because it requires you to have a strong connection to your intuition. Other times, you won't receive a direct response, but will instead receive a clue. Remember, spirit guides are powerful beings with their own personalities. Calling on them will not necessarily make them want to reveal themselves to you straight away. Often, by concealing themselves and making you work to discover them, you learn important lessons along the way.

One relatively simple way of contacting your spirit guides is through visualisation. There are quite a few spirit guide visualisations already out there on the internet, which you could try. You might even like to create your own visualisation by listening to soothing music and imagining that you are walking down a dark staircase into a white room. Remember to always set an intention for your visualisation. In this case, it would be, "I wish to connect with my spirit guide", or something similar.

A trance is similar to meditation. No... this doesn't refer to a genre of music, but to a state of mind, as in, a half-conscious state. You know that strange mental space you enter before you go to sleep, which is technically called the hypnogogic state? That is the state we're aiming for. When you are in a trance, your mind is open and receptive. It no longer has the typical filters of conscious waking reality. As such, this state is perfect for connecting with your spirit guides.

Many ancient cultures used trance to 'connect with the gods.' Different ways of entering into a trance include self-hypnosis, various breathing exercises, relaxation techniques, watching a pendulum, visualisation, drumming and even dancing.

Nature immersion is another safe way to contact your guides. When you take the time to look and pay attention, nature can become sublimely magical. It is also a beautiful place to come in contact with your spirit guides, particularly an animal spirit. Find some place outside in a park, by a river or stream or while going on a hike. Look at the clouds, the bodies of water and trees. Can you glimpse any figures or faces? What animals keep appearing that have seemed to accompany you for a while?

Synchronicity is another word for meaningful coincidence. Looking for synchronicities are an important aspect in communicating with our guides. Have you ever seen repetitive numbers (such as 3333, 1111, 1212), names, or symbols arise in your life? Is so, then pay attention since these often carry important messages. In order to use the synchronicity technique for contacting your spirit guides, set an intention. Praying is a good way to do this. Here is an example, "Dear God, if it is your will, please help me discover my spirit guides.

Please send me signs each day that I can understand. Thank you. Amen."

Keep a look out every day for unusual and repetitious signs, names, symbols, places or objects that appear. Keep a notebook and record your observations, and reflect on what you have seen after one week. Have you been shown something? Synchronicity works best when we are in touch with our inner selves, so ensure that you are practicing mindful awareness. An in-depth exploration of synchronicities will be discussed in the 'synchronicity' chapter.

Now that you understand the different kinds of good souls and spirits that surround you, there is no need to be afraid of the spiritual world, as long as you know how to stay protected. It's great to have a connection to that world, because it helps us become better people here on earth, to love and be kind, and also to appreciate the smallest of things. Many spirits are there to transform us and make us better souls.

Unfortunately, there are some negative spirits that don't want that to happen. But with will-power, strength and spiritual connection, we can overcome most negative spirits as well as any negative obstacles in life. Knowing safe ways in which you can contact your spirit guides will see you on a path to enhanced spirituality, and have you more connected than you ever imagined possible.

The next chapter discusses the controversial topic of 'reincarnation'.

CHAPTER NINE

◆

Reincarnation

What exactly is reincarnation or rebirth? It's the philosophical or religious concept that the nonphysical essence of a living being starts a new life in a different physical form after biological death.

Depending upon the accumulation of karma, from what I have learnt through spiritual guides and intuition, rebirth occurs into a higher or lower bodily form, either in heaven or hell, or even in the earthly realm. No physical bodily form is permanent, everyone dies and only some reincarnate further to live in a new form in order to learn lessons that they perhaps did not learn well in their previous life.

REINCARNATION

While the belief in reincarnation is most characteristic of South Asian and East Asian traditions, it also appears in the religious and philosophical thought of local religions, in some ancient Middle Eastern religions (eg: the Greek Orphic mystery, or salvation religion), Manichaeism, and Gnosticism, as well as in such modern religious movements as Theosophy.

In many local religions, belief in multiple souls is common. The soul is frequently viewed as being capable of leaving the body through the mouth or the nostrils and of being reborn, for example, as a bird, a butterfly, or an insect. The Venda of Southern Africa believe that, when a person dies, the soul stays near the grave for a short time and then seeks a new resting place or inhabits another human, mammalian, or reptilian body.

Development of the notion of transmigration is common in Indian philosophy. The hymns may, in general, be said to express a positive attitude toward human life and to show interest. Among the ancient Greeks, the Orphic mystery religion held that a pre-existent soul survives bodily death and is later reincarnated into a human or other mammalian body. It eventually receives release from the cycle of birth and death and regains its former pure state. Plato, in the 5th–4th century BCE, believed in an immortal soul that participates in frequent incarnations.

The major religions that hold a belief in reincarnation however, are mostly Asian religions, especially Hinduism, Jainism, Buddhism and Sikhism, all of which arose in India. They all hold in common a doctrine of karma, the law of cause and effect, which states that what one does in this present life will have an effect in the next life.

In Hinduism, the process of birth and rebirth, that is the transmigration of souls, is endless until one achieves 'moksha', or liberation from that process. Moksha is achieved when one realises that the eternal core of the individual (atman) and the absolute reality (Brahman) are one. Thus, one can escape from the process of death and rebirth (samsara).

Jainism reflects a belief in an eternal and transmigrating life principle (jiva), that is akin to an individual soul, and holds that karma is a fine particulate substance that settles upon the jiva according to the deeds that a person does. Thus, the burden of the old karma is added to the new karma that is acquired during the next existence until the jiva frees itself by religious disciplines, especially by 'ahimsa' (non-violence). Then it can rise to the place of liberated jivas at the top of the universe.

Although Buddhism denies the existence of an unchanging, substantial soul or self, as against the notion of the atman it teaches the concept of 'anatman' (or the non-self). It holds to a belief in the transmigration of the karma that is accumulated by an individual in life.

The individual is a composition of five ever-changing psycho-physical elements and states, or 'skandhas' (bundles); form, sensations, perceptions, impulses, and consciousness, which terminates in death. The karma of the deceased however, persists and becomes a 'vijnana' (germ of consciousness) in the womb of a mother. The vijnana is that aspect of consciousness that is reborn in a new individual. By gaining a state of complete passiveness through discipline and meditation, one can achieve nirvana, the state of the extinction of desires and liberation (moksha) from bondage to samsara by karma.

Sikhism teaches a doctrine of reincarnation based on the Hindu view, but in addition holds that after the Last Judgment, souls that have been reincarnated in several existences will be absorbed in God.

I'd like to talk about my own experiences with reincarnation. There once was a woman named Shanti Devi, who was an Indian woman who had claimed to remember her past life. Shanti was born on the eleventh of December 1926 and died in 1987. This woman became the subject of reincarnation research, which was set up by Mahatma Gandhi who was an Indian political leader who supported her claim. There are many books about Shanti Devi, though I will tell you what I know.

This lady, whose picture I touched to gain my own personal insight into her truth, was amazing. Shanti stated that as a little girl she started to remember some details of a past life that she had lived and according to those accounts she explained to her mother at four years of age that her real home was actually in Mathura where her husband lived, which was not far from where she currently lived in Delhi.

She felt that her parents thought she was slightly crazy and decided to run away from home at age six, trying to make it back to her home in Mathura. At the school she attended, she told her teachers that she was married and that she had died ten days after giving birth to her child. She was interviewed by the headmaster over these statements and claimed that her husband's name was "Kedar Nath".

The headmaster managed to locate a man of that name who revealed how he had lost his wife, Lugdi Devi, nine years earlier, 10 days after giving birth to a son. Kedar Nath then travelled to Delhi to meet Shanti and pretended to be his own brother, though Shanti recognised him straight away. She also knew several details of Kedar's wife that were impossible for her to know. So, he became convinced that she was the reincarnation of Lugdi Devi.

After I had engaged in a reading of my own, I found that everything she had said was in fact the truth. My spiritual guides inserted a video of her two lives in my mind, and it was amazing to learn of her story. Just like Shanti, there are many others who can make similar claims of earlier lives.

Her story finally reached Mahatma Gandhi, who set up a commission to investigate. The commission travelled with Shanti to Mathura around 1935, and what happened next astounded me, for she recognised a few of Lugdi's former family members and stated their names and their relationship to the deceased woman. How could such a young child who had never been there know all that?

First, she recognised Lugdi's grandfather. She also came to realise that Kedar Nath had neglected to keep many of the last wishes that Lugdi had asked for while on her death bed. The commission's final report was that she was indeed the reincarnation of Lugdi Devi. Shanti went on to tell her story many more times until her second death in 1987.

The second time around, was heaven her final destination, or who or what might she be now? According to my guides from the spirit world, her time on earth had been served. On one hand I feel blessed to be able to accumulate all of this information, but why would one want to know their fate or destiny? The unknown is much more satisfying, so remember that, the next time you consider seeing a psychic to reveal your future. If you want to speak with a loved one, by all means go ahead as that is truly an amazing experience and a sense of closure, but I suggest you leave your future as a surprise.

Every religion has a different belief, but from my spiritual experiences and connections to the spirit world, Buddha is in my opinion, the most enlightened way for me. As we know, Buddhists believe that death is a natural part of the life cycle. They believe that death leads to rebirth while the spirit remains close by and seeks out a new body and life, which is somewhat comforting. However, their stay in what is known as heaven is not eternal because they eventually use up all of their good karma and must therefore undergo rebirth into another realm, as a human, animal or other being to earn more karma. However, despite my many connections, I haven't encountered a soul being reborn into an animal yet.

They say heaven is temporary and part of what they call a 'samsara'. Buddhists focus more on escaping the cycle of rebirth and reaching enlightenment known as 'nirvana'. One soul would have to be as pure as gold to achieve this state, such as the Dalai Lama, who belongs to the Gelugpa tradition of Tibetan Buddhism, which is the largest and most influential tradition in Tibet.

I am a Christian and I know that Jesus saved me from my turmoil, and that he existed and was a very special man with many special abilities and powers. Buddhism is rather different to Christianity. One element being that while Christianity is monotheistic at its core and relies on a God as a creator, Buddhism is generally non-theistic and rejects the notion of a creator god, which provides divine values for the world.

While I am unsure of Earth's creator and God, I know Jesus is watching over all of us and as long as we have faith and don't deny him, we will reach heaven. Though according to Buddha, this destination will not be eternal. I don't say this because I am a religious freak. I actually despise religion and all the horror and catastrophes that it causes. I do not believe the majority of the writings in the bible, but I will not deny Jesus, since this man eliminated a demon from my soul. How can I deny him or the exorcism that happened in front of my very own eyes?

I feel Buddhists are precisely right in their theory of the afterlife. This is a result of my own spiritual connections and guidance and negative experiences. I don't know if they are wrong about there being a higher power, I guess I will see that for myself when my time comes. It is all so confusing at times. But I have endured many spiritual insights and experiences in accumulating the knowledge that I now possess, and am able to share.

Although I can't elaborate on each and every one of the previous lives I have already lived, since my ability hasn't allowed me to see into all of them yet, I do have an interesting experience with reincarnation. According to my five spiritual guides, which I have with me most of the time, I was an Italian artist in one previous life. I lived in Milan with three children, but I died of lung cancer at the age of 43. That is all I know because that's all they gave me, but the fact that I have apparently lived 14 times in total shows I still have yet to learn many more things here on Earth.

Will this present one be my last life? Probably not, though I pray that my soul is wanting to reach the state of enlightenment, or nirvana as they call it, but as sappy as it sounds, one's soul must be pure to achieve this destiny.

The Dalai Lama speaks of many truths such as: "Happiness is not something ready-made, it comes from your own actions"; and "Love is the absence of judgement"; "My religion is very simple, it's the religion of kindness"; "Love and compassion are necessities, not luxuries, without them humanity cannot survive".

And my favourite Dalai Lama quote is: "Every day, think as you wake up... today I am fortunate to be alive, I have a precious human life, I am not going to waste it. I am going to use all my energies to develop myself, to extend my heart out to others, and to achieve enlightenment for the benefit of all beings. I am going to have kind thoughts towards others, I am not going to get angry or think badly about others. I am going to benefit others as much as I can".

With those words, I believe this man will reach enlightenment and will not ever experience rebirth again. And I believe this is also true of Jesus, he will also live eternally up in the heavens and welcome us if we do the same. I know in this day and age it can be difficult to act that way all of the time, but the thing is we must at least try for it would make the world such a better place and that is all Jesus wants.

You don't have to believe what I am telling you. I understand that it is hard to grasp since you probably, and hopefully, haven't had the experiences I have had in order to find Jesus. Though, if you do or already believe he exists you are forever loved and safe, this I know.

Knowing my beliefs regarding reincarnation, some might wonder how they can find what their own past lives were. There are signs to look for that may indicate that you are a reincarnated soul.

You might have a powerful intuition. People who have reincarnated just seem to have an ability to know things before the rest of us. They can go deep within to access knowledge otherwise hidden to others and have a way of sensing things before they happen. Intuitive souls may have connections to other dimensions and worlds and have the ability to talk to beings from other dimensions. They spend a lot of time in quietude, mulling over the information they have been given and trying to make sense of it all.

Another sign is that you may regularly experience 'déjà vu'. If you have lived before this life, you may have an eerie sense that certain events have happened to you before. For example, if you take a road trip across the country and feel as though you have driven those exact roads even though you haven't. This may indicate that you have been here at one point in time in another form. Certain people, places or events may seem oddly familiar to you, even if you can't remember seeing or meeting them before.

You might be extremely sensitive. Reincarnated souls have a high level of sensitivity and empathy. They feel everything to the core and feel that they have a mission in life to help bring peace and healing to the planet. They have a very hard time dealing with the conflicting and turbulent energies of the world sometimes, and need a lot of time to rebalance themselves. Empathic people hate being in crowded, noisy places and often avoid them as much as possible.

You may feel as though you don't belong. A reincarnated soul sometimes feels out of place here on Earth. They search forever for their home, but can't find it. They feel like an alien here, just watching in perplexity as people go about their daily lives. They can't seem to understand why or how, and don't have any desire to engage in 'normal' activities. They would rather spend time alone just lying under the stars, contemplating life and avoiding things that don't have meaning to them. Reincarnated souls have a deep longing to connect once again with their soul family and have a hard time fitting in or feeling comforted on this planet.

You might have a strong urge to travel somewhere in particular. You might have memories of living in a certain country or city in a past life and have an insatiable desire to go there once again, in this life. You have a wandering soul, and because you realise that home isn't a physical place, but a feeling in your heart, you want to go anywhere and everywhere on this Earth.

However, you might feel drawn to a particular location or culture, possibly because you lived there in a past life. Don't hesitate to immerse yourself in a new land or way of living; you might take away valuable lessons about yourself and your soul's mission.

The most obvious sign would be that you have memories of a past life. You can't shake the feeling that you've lived here before, and the memories might come to you in your dreams, through a song on the radio, a line in a book, or some other mysterious way. However, you don't recall these events or people from a past lifetime, so you can't quite place these memories on a timeline. You just know they happened and wish to uncover more about your past lives. Children can usually recall more about their previous existences because they have just come from a past incarnation.

MEDITATION

Meditation is certainly a useful practice tool for looking into reincarnation. You can turn to meditation in order to connect with your past life. Note that this may need some practice, for one time might not be enough to open yourself and connect to your past lives.

First, find a quiet room where you will not be disturbed. Make sure you will be comfortable and remove any outside distractions, eg: turn off your phone, computer and television. If other people are around, politely ask them to refrain from disturbing you. You may find it useful to have some calm music playing very softly in the background, so choose something that resembles the sound of waves or a waterfall. Sit down, make yourself comfortable and close your eyes. Turning off the lights and closing the curtains may also be a good idea. You may even prefer to lie down, if this will help you relax more.

In your mind, imagine yourself in a long hallway, with a door at the far end. Focus on the details of what it looks like and remember these details, as each time you want to look into your past lives, this is where you will begin. The hallway can appear however you want it to look. It can be richly decorated or plain, a castle or cathedral, or even a forest path. The choice is entirely yours.

Making sure you visualise this in as much detail as possible, walk down the hallway, paying attention as your feet move along the ground. You visualise what the journey looks like. Take note of the appearance, sounds, colours and even the smells. Then, once you reach the door, open it.

The first thing you see on the other side of the door, whatever it may be, is something from one of your previous lives. It may turn out to be a very specific item, or you might be visualising something more abstract, such as a colour. Keep going, carry on moving forwards, and your vision will become clearer and more detailed. Be patient. If this is your first time trying to search for past lives, then you may find that it takes a while for the details to become clear. Ask yourself questions like, why do you like a particular hobby, a place or even a song? Could it be related to a past life? The answer could be yes, and asking this question may lead you to that information.

You will reach a point where the visions stop moving, at which time you open your eyes and bring yourself back to the present moment. Normally, this will occur once you have been exploring your past life for a while. However, if you wish to remove yourself from the visions before they stop, imagine yourself walking back up the hallway to where you started.

The concept of reincarnation and past lives is complex, but through guided meditation there is little else you need to start your journey into your past lives. Karma from our past lives is often brought to us in this life and it affects us in ways we don't even know. Going through a past life regression may help you understand what has happened and how it affects your current life. This can help you to learn and may remove any bad karma put onto your life in the past, so that you may live a happy, beautiful life going forward.

---◆---

CHAPTER TEN

How to Keep the Soul Strong

Having covered the positive and negative souls, with the latter being mainly demons, it is important to understand how you can protect yourself against the negative and awful energy of evil demons.

PREVENTING POSSESSION

The main thing to prevent yourself from being possessed is to never allow yourself to become vulnerable, by remaining positive at all times. Even if you are wasted from drugs or alcohol, or feeling extremely anxious or depressed, it is important to remain positive and not allow yourself to slip into a state of depression. I know life is not as simple as that, but the higher your energy level, the less likely a demon will be able to attach itself to you. Remember, the energy you put out, is the same energy you will receive. In a later chapter, this narrative covers in more depth the concept of 'manifestation', which examines how your energy output attracts similar energy throughout your life.

Low energy levels tend to open up your soul to potential demonic attacks, although not everyone will encounter a demon or ever have an issue, but it is possible. In Australia alone there have been over 50,000 demonic oppression and possession cases. I became one of those unfortunate people who had to experience this terrifying phenomenon. Before that occurred, I was also a person that thought that such an event could never happen to me. I barely even believed that demons were amongst us. Try the following effective methods of preventing demonic possession to keep yourself and your family safe.

If you detect that a demon is in your home, but not yet attached to your soul, pour salt in every corner of your home before bedtime. This puts demons to sleep for the night so you can't be harmed until morning. In the morning, waste no time in seeking a bishop's assistance. Also, sprinkle holy water from your local church in every room and ask Jesus for his protection. Demons don't like holy water because it burns them.

STONES AND CRYSTALS

The next section of this book concentrates on strengthening the soul through the positive energy emitted by crystals, through mindfulness, as well as other positive effects and advantages that they confer.

There is varying support for crystals with some saying they have limited use, while others insist they have genuine healing properties. Whichever side you're on, all the evidence agrees that they are becoming very popular. There are countless minerals produced in the pressurised womb of Mother Earth, which rise to the surface to become crystals, where they can share their insight and their healing magic. They are known as ancient spiritual healing tools.

What is well known is that everything on Earth is comprised of energy, so why would rocks, gems and crystals be any different? Each crystal has their individual signature energy field and those energy vibrations interact with our own energetic vibrations, which in turn, directly affects our physical and emotional self.

Believe it or not, these beautiful and ancient crystals are available to support us and can even call to us when we are in need of their healing properties.

If you're just beginning to use crystals, a great way to harness their healing power is by using healing stones for manifesting your goals and what you intend to create in your life. When it comes to crystal basics, these amazing rocks connect us to the Earth because they are tangible, physical forms that possess powerful vibrations. This energy continues to connect with you when you wear these 'intention crystals' close to the skin or place them nearby in your environment. With every thought and intention, these crystals pick up on your unique vibrational energy and amplify the positive vibes that you're cultivating.

In this magical world of vibrations, crystal energy helps you on your spiritual journey because it works to hold your intention and remind you of your connection to the Earth. A well thought out intention is the starting point for healing crystals because specific intentions instilled into your daily thought patterns also become part of its energy.

One of the first pieces of scientific evidence relating to the power of crystals was the work done by IBM scientist Marcel Vogel. While watching crystals grow under a microscope, he noticed that their shape took the form of whatever he was thinking about. He hypothesised that these vibrations were the result of the constant assembling and disassembling of bonds between molecules. He also tested the metaphysical power of quartz crystal and proved that rocks can store thoughts similar to the way tapes use magnetic energy to record sound.

Albert Einstein said everything in life is vibration, and just like sound waves, your thoughts match the vibrations of everything that manifests in your life. Therefore, if you think crystals have healing potential, the positive vibes of the stones will amplify those thoughts.

At every moment, we have the ability to choose our thoughts and as we continue our journey, each day presents us with new challenges and wonderful beginnings. Healing crystals remind us to quiet the chatter of the mind and reconnect to the universally healing vibrations of the Earth. An important lesson to learn from crystals is patience, because just like the eons of time it took for these semi-precious stones to evolve and transform, working with the healing power of crystals also takes time.

As you learn, grow and evolve, use crystals as a reminder to be grateful for the abundance of Mother Nature and the great mysteries of the universe. Below is a list of 20 of the most important and powerful rock crystals, where they come from and what they are used for.

1. Selenite - THE MASTER
This crystal is the only one that doesn't need to be charged and is actually capable of recharging other crystals. It is found in salt lakes and can be found from Mexico to Brazil. The healing properties in this crystal create the highest level of consciousness and all that is infinite, such as your spirit guides and intuition. This stone can bring the spirit world to Earth and remind us where we come from. These things are known as 'metaphysical'. The physical healing properties in this crystal bring great healing and inner peace if you carry it with you at all times.

2. Moonstone - THE STABILISER
This crystal is linked to the feminine and the moon. It creates harmony within and strengthens one's intuition. It was the stone of gods and goddesses in India and is very sacred. Metaphysical properties in this stone can open you up to their worlds and also manages the ego and materialism of a soul. I can think of a few people who could use this one! Regarding the physical, healing side of this stone, it is capable of helping with the digestive system, water retention, hormonal problems, menstrual issues and obesity. The last three apply to me and it is now time to invest in a few crystals for myself.

3. Aventurine - THE STONE OF OPPORTUNITY
This is my favourite stone, responsible for improving your luck and opportunity, prosperity and abundance. This is a good stone to have if you head to Crown Casino or to the local newsagent to invest in a Tatts ticket. These crystals are the 'metaphysical' type, once again, and their physical healing properties are very supportive

of the heart, blood and energy circulation and help speed up recovery time after an injury.

4. Crystal Quartz - THE SPIRIT STONE

This stone is the most common type. It is known as the window of light into the metaphysical world. It contains the entire colour spectrum and can be used to amplify desires, prayers and manifestations from the spirit world to the physical world. So, of course I regularly have a few of these under my pillow and in my pockets. They are good to meditate with, and increase the manifestations of your desires. On the physical healing side, it is a master healer, stimulating the immune system and increasing energy levels.

5. Citrine - THE MONEY STONE

This is a type of quartz. It is a golden, yellow crystal which is associated with a connection to money and wealth. Its metaphysical healing properties include stability and financial wealth if you take it with you to work, sit it on your desk and stare at it as much as you can throughout the day. The physical healing properties of citrine are known to stimulate the metabolism and eliminate nausea. It is also associated with the strengthening of nerve impulses, helping the brain to fire more rapidly.

6. Agate - STONE OF INNER STABILITY

This stone comes in all colours. Agate embodies our inner world. Metaphysically, agate raises self-awareness, stabilises the aura and transforms negative energy. This stone heals the angry and emotionally unstable. The physical properties are known to improve mental function by improving clarity and thought.

7. Tourmaline - THE GROUNDING STONE

This stone is used as a psychic shield to ground your energy and combat the entry of negative entities into your energy field. It can be found on every continent, so get your hands on a few and pass them around. The metaphysical healing properties in this stone are the fact that it acts as a sponge to capture negative entities and encourages you to remain radiant during dark times. The physical healing properties in this crystal ease pain in the joints and assists in realigning the spine. It also releases tension.

8. Rose Quartz - THE LOVE STONE

Most people's favourite, this pink quartz represents love and is associated with the heart and with expressing unconditional love to yourself and others. This is a unique and great stone to help invite love into your life. Its metaphysical properties help attract your soulmate since this stone is all about the matters of the heart. It will either deepen an existing love or help you to find love if it's worn around the neck. The physical healing properties in this stone improve circulation and blood pressure and also eases palpitations. This crystal is centred around the heart chakra.

9. Turquoise - THE STONE OF PROTECTION

This stone is believed to be the oldest crystal known to mankind. It is a sign of wisdom. Turquoise is prevalent in almost all ancient cultures and has always been known as the stone of protection. The metaphysical healing properties in this stone strengthen the meridians in the body and supports intuition and meditation. Because it is blue, it is associated with the throat chakra which creates clear communication. On the physical healing side, it assists with problems in the brain, ears, neck, and throat. It is known to clear blockages.

10. Fluorite - THE STONE OF POSITIVITY

This crystal is one of the most powerful. It is known to suck any negative energy right out of you like a leach. It creates room for light to shine in on you. This is a magical crystal. Its metaphysical healing properties are used to protect your aura, raise vibrations and protect you from a chaotic mind. This stone is a rainbow colour and is mainly used to stabilise the mind, intensify psychic connections and heighten intuitive powers. The physical healing properties in this crystal help you to clear the mind and sharpen your focus. It can also ease cold and flu symptoms. Perhaps with Corona virus going around at this present time these beauties may come in handy.

11. Lapis Lazuli - THE STONE OF TRUTH

Blue is the colour of this gorgeous stone. It is vibrant and very sought after. It is associated with royalty and luxury. It also instils us with wisdom and good judgement. The metaphysical healing properties that are received from this stone are the activation of the upper chakras, empowered communication, and the ability to speak our truths. It also helps us discover the spirit realm. The physical healing properties of this crystal include the healing of the throat and vocal cords, since it has strong ties to the brain.

12. Hematite - THE GROUNDING STONE

This stone is enriched with iron and is very connected to the earth. Some call it the bloodstone in Greece, because it is red and red also represents the Earth. The metaphysical healing properties of this stone are connected to the root chakra and have a strong energy that reminds us of our human existence and supports us financially. Its physical healing properties include improvement of the blood stream and support of a healthy heart. It also alleviates stress and calms the nervous system.

13. Jade - THE DREAM STONE

This stone can be found in many colours, around the world. The region actually dictates the colour. It was one of the most commonly used stones in ancient times. Jade's metaphysical healing properties are connected to the heart. It helps us to accept truth and express love to others. It also assists in accessing shamanic realms in the dream state. Its physical healing properties are associated with the heart. Jade is good for filtering out toxins and cleansing the body and it eases joint pain and speeds up healing.

14. Amethyst - THE MANIFESTATION STONE

This stone is common amongst the new-age, along with selenite and crystal quartz. Amethysts can be found worldwide. This gorgeous purple stone holds manifestation at the top of its list. Its metaphysical healing properties connect you to your heart's wants and needs. It helps you to discover your life purpose and then manifests those goals in your life. This stone affects the upper chakras, helping us bring the spiritual realm to the physical plane. This stone can also help with bringing our dreams to life, here on Earth. The crystal's physical healing properties can be used to boost your nervous system, balance hormones, reduce headaches, ease neck tension and decrease insomnia. I suggest you sleep with an amethyst under your pillow to wake fully refreshed.

15. Kyanite - THE STONE OF EMOTION

Kyanite helps us to create a pathway where there wasn't one before, in terms of emotional development and meditation. This stone doesn't accumulate negative energy, so it doesn't need to be cleansed. The blue-green colour is associated with the sky, so it creates serenity and peace and soothes the nerves. Your natural psychic ability can be enhanced with this stone for it deepens meditation and opens up channels to the spirit world. This stone's physical healing properties help heal almost any pain in the throat and improve communication. It also eases facial tension.

16. Obsidian - THE MIRROR STONE

This stone is jet black and helps to improve sight and the way you see the world, as it acts as a mirror. It allows you to look deeply within yourself to reveal your true spirit. Back in the Stone Age they used this stone to gain an insight into other worlds, into the soul itself, and into other realms that aren't accessible from Earth to gain wisdom and knowledge. Use this stone's metaphysical healing properties to reveal the shadow self. Obsidian's physical healing properties relieve emotional distress that has long been buried deep down inside your soul, ignored, or forgotten. This helps ease any life trauma you may have experienced.

17. Blue Topaz - THE STONE OF CREATIVITY

This stone is bright, beautiful blue and reflects the mind and our true potential for creativity. It opens the mind to new ideas. Its metaphysical healing properties help connect you to your angels and also passed loved ones. Use this stone to enhance the true power of the mind and align with the spirit world. The physical healing properties of Topaz are known to assist with mental illness. It also assists with diseases of the eyes and restores loss of taste.

18. Opal - THE EYE STONE

This stone looks like it is on fire, with a rainbow spectrum of electric colours. It is associated with the eye since it is beautiful to look at and it is associated with the third eye chakra. Opal inspires optimism, happiness and appreciation. There are over ten different types of opal, each with slightly different properties. The metaphysical healing properties of Opal bring light into the whole aura. It can amplify a vibrant energy in the soul. Its physical healing properties help heal the eyes or improve vision. It can also assist with memory.

19. Amazonite - STONE OF COURAGE

This stone calms the spirit and soothes the soul with its cool, greenish colour. Amazonite makes you seek and express your inner truths with conviction. Its metaphysical healing properties are used to balance and cleanse the chakras. It also soothes trauma stored in the body and helps prevent the manifestation of this trauma from turning into a physical illness. Amazonite's physical healing properties are used for general well-being. It assists the whole body.

20. Garnet - THE STONE OF HEALTH AND CREATIVITY
This is a grounding stone and is found in many colours. It's commonly known for its qualities of promoting health and the flow of creativity. Garnet's metaphysical healing properties help to remove inhibitions and taboos and allows the mind to think freely. It invites your own spirit to participate in the physical world and opens up channels of creativity. You might like the sound of this stone as its physical healing properties assist with one's metabolism and stimulates it. Its purpose is to get things in the body moving. It also assists with blood flow and sexual desire.

There are more crystals, but the above 20 crystals are the most powerful stones. They can be found in crystal and jewellery stores. They are also available through Target stores or places online such as E-bay and Amazon. Identifying the different crystals and understanding their purpose is important but users should also know how to take care of crystals and recharge them.

CLEANING CRYSTALS

Healing crystals need to be cleansed occasionally, but why is cleansing necessary? Crystals often travel long distances, from the source to the seller, before a purchase is made. Each transition exposes the stone to various energies that may be misaligned with your own. And when used for healing, these stones are said to absorb or redirect the negativity that you're working to release. Regularly cleansing and recharging your stones is the only way to restore your crystal to its natural state. A by-product of this act of care can be to also reinvigorate your own sense of purpose. Some of the most common techniques for cleansing crystals, and how to align a crystal with your intention, are as follows:

Running water. Pure fresh running water is said to neutralise any negative energy stored inside the stone and return it back to the Earth. Although natural running water, like a stream, is best, you can also rinse your stone under a tap. Whatever your water source, ensure that your stone is completely submerged. Allow approximately one minute of cleansing per stone. Pat it dry when finished. Use this method for hard stones such as quartz. Don't use this procedure for stones that are brittle or soft.

Saltwater. Salt has been used throughout history to absorb unwanted energy and banish negativity. If you're near the ocean, consider collecting a bowl of fresh saltwater. Otherwise, mix a tablespoon of sea, rock, or table salt into a bowl of water. Make sure that your stone is completely submerged and allow it to soak for a few hours to a few days' time. Rinse and pat dry when complete. Approximate duration of treatment: up to 48 hours. Use this for hard stones, such as quartz and amethyst. Don't use this for stones that are soft, porous, or contain traces of metal.

Brown rice. This method can also be used to draw out negativity in a safe and contained setting. It is especially beneficial for protective stones, such as black tourmaline. The procedure is to fill a bowl with dry brown rice and bury your stone beneath the grains. Dispose of the rice immediately after the cleansing, since the rice is said to have absorbed the energy you're trying to eradicate. Approximate duration of treatment is 24 hours. Use this method for any type of stone.

Natural light. Although ritual cleansing is often centred around certain points in the solar or lunar cycle, you can set your stone out at any time to cleanse and recharge. Set your stone out before nightfall and plan to bring it in before 11am. This will allow your stone to bathe in the light of both the moon and the sun. Prolonged exposure to direct sunlight may weather the stone's surface, so make sure you collect it up again in the morning.

If you're able to, place your stone directly on the Earth. This will allow for further cleansing. Wherever you lay them, ensure they won't be disturbed by wildlife or passers-by. Afterwards, give the stone a quick rinse to remove any dirt and debris. Pat it dry. The approximate duration of treatment is 10 to 12 hours. Use this for most tumbled stones. Don't use this for vibrant stones, such as amethyst. Note that soft stones can be damaged by inclement weather.

Visualisation. Although this is considered the safest way to clear stones, it can be intimidating for some. The more in tune you are with your sense of self, the easier it may be to redirect your energy to the stone you want to restore. Take a few minutes to ground and centre your energy, then pick up your stone and visualise your hands filling with white, radiant light. See this light surround the stone and feel it growing brighter in your hands. Envision the impurities flushing out of the stone, allowing the stone to shine brighter with renewed purpose. Continue this visualisation until you feel a shift in the stone's energy. Approximate duration of treatment is about one minute per stone. Use this cleansing method for any type of stone.

The more often you use a stone, the more energy it collects. A good rule of thumb is to clear all of your stones at least once a month. If an individual stone is feeling heavier than usual, go ahead and cleanse it. You don't have to wait a designated amount of time between clearings. How do you activate your crystal if it feels heavier than expected, like it's lost its shine? It may benefit from a little energetic activation.

Try lending it some of your own energy by speaking to it, singing to it, or sending it some vital life force energy through your breath. A little interaction can go a long way! If you have plans outside, consider taking the stone out with you. Many people find that allowing the stone to soak up natural energy at the park or beach has a powerful effect.

You can also create an activation grid by surrounding the stone with its more energetic counterparts. Popular choices include ruby, clear quartz, apophyllite, kyanite, selenite, and carnelian. You can use whatever stones you're drawn towards. Just make sure they fully surround the target crystal so that it can completely bask in their vibrations.

Now that you know about a few crystals, how to use them, clear them and activate them, you can go out and buy your first crystal and start your crystal journey. They're both beautiful to collect and they help with healing, empowering and even bringing luck!

CHAPTER ELEVEN

◆

Seance

What is a séance? A séance is a meeting at which people try communicating with individuals who have passed on, and it is usually performed through a medium. Séance is the French word for 'session'.

Throughout the 19th century, séances were the 'in' thing to do. Hosts would gather individuals together to communicate with the dead. However, scepticism has grown strong against séances in more recent years, and nowadays we rarely see individuals taking part in any sessions. Some may believe it to be an invitation to evil because you're opening a portal which you may not be able to close. However, some believe that séances are a beautiful thing, because one gets to speak to loved ones that have passed on, or even friendly ghosts that are trying to guide you through life. How is a séance performed?

If you're thinking about having a séance, you'll need to find like-minded individuals and the right paraphernalia. When choosing guests to take part in your séance, you should try to select individuals who are open to the idea of contacting the dead. Any sceptics that may be present can harm the likelihood of the séance being successful. You should definitely leave children out of any séance because the experience may be too intense and overwhelming. The paraphernalia you will need for the session includes a round table, candles and food since these items are believed to attract warm spirits.

Let's describe how you perform a séance and increase the chances of contact. The first thing you'll need to do is to assemble your participants in the place where you'll be doing the séance. Some say that the number of participants should be divisible by three, but this isn't a hard and fast rule. No fewer than three people should perform a séance, as it can be emotionally and physically exhausting on a small group of individuals.

You will need to use a round or oval table. Why is that important? This helps to create a symbolic circle, which is a shape normally represented in rituals. Additionally, this also helps the group to hold hands. This is another important aspect of a séance. Holding hands creates a stronger energy, which is shared amongst the group.

Once everyone is assembled around a round table, you'll need to pick your medium. The medium is the main person who will conduct the séance, and is usually the person through whom questions are asked. Your medium must be the person with the most experience with doing séances, or a person who has psychic abilities. This is an important step, because a medium conducting the séance needs to be able to successfully reach out to the spirits on the other side of the veil.

Next, you will have to set up the table appropriately. In the centre of the table, place natural food. A good food to use would be bread or soup, as they have a natural aroma. Food in a séance is said to attract spirits who are in need of physical nourishment. After you've placed the food on the table, you should light candles. Once again, place a number of candles that can be divisible by three. You should also have no fewer than three candles, and the more the merrier. This helps attract spirits who seek warmth and comfort. Additionally, candles create a strong energy in the room. Spirits need a large amount of energy to contact individuals. Having a lot of energy in the room can help them absorb the energy in order to communicate effectively.

After you've successfully lit your candles, you'll need to create a calming ambience. You can do this by dimming your lights, turning off any music and eliminate distractions, because you'll need to concentrate.

Now we're onto the step of summoning the spirit. All the individuals around the table need to join their hands and summon the spirit. All participants should chant the same words, and a good chant goes something like this:

"Our beloved (name of spirit), we bring you gifts from life to death. Communicate with us (name of spirit) and move amongst us."

You should now patiently wait for a response. It is important to remain open and patient. If the spirit hasn't contacted you, the group should repeat the chant until the spirit feels comfortable enough to communicate. Understand that spirits can communicate in different ways. You don't necessarily have to hear them speak to you. They could communicate by knocking or by communicating psychically through the medium.

Once the spirit responds to your chant, begin gently by asking your questions. You should ask common questions that can be answered by a simple YES or NO. If the spirit responds by knocking or any type of noise, ask them to communicate by knocking once for NO and twice for YES. This gives you and the spirit some clarity and direction. If the spirit decides to communicate with you directly, through the medium, you can ask them any type of question and won't be limited by a YES or NO response.

Sometimes séances can become overwhelming and intense. If this is the case, it's important to remain in control and end the séance. It is highly important to end a séance affectively. If done wrong, the spirit can linger around. You wouldn't want this if you've contacted a rebellious or malicious spirit.

How do you end a séance correctly? You should thank the spirit for communicating with you and tell them they can go in peace. You should then break the joining of your hands, extinguish the candles and turn on the lights. It's important to realise that holding a séance can at times be very emotional. Therefore, you should proceed with caution and patience. You should not make a joke out of it as you can easily offend the spirit.

There are terrifying stories about séances that have gone wrong, so it is important to understand the positives and negatives of holding a séance. These bad events generally arise where the portal between the real world and the spirit world hasn't been closed properly, and had some post-séance tag-alongs. While some spirits that attach themselves to you can become negative, they seem to have good intentions. Remember that spirits are usually lingering around because they're attached to the real world.

However, these manifestations can range in intensity, from subtle to extreme, depending on the spirit you've contacted. Some have reported manifestations of malevolent spirits and others report full-blown demonic infestation. Although, this is not as common as ghosts who believe they've been invited to infiltrate the life and the homes of those who have summoned them. Their presence can however, become negative.

Whether these reports are true or not, séances haven't earned a good reputation over the years. What does the Bible say about contacting the dead? Deuteronomy 18:10-12 made the following instruction:

"There should not be found in you anyone who employs divination, anyone practicing magic, anyone who looks for omens, a sorcerer, anyone binding others with a spell, anyone who consults a spirit medium or a fortune-teller, or anyone who inquires of the dead. For whoever does these things is detestable to Jehovah."

This verse is referring to pagan beliefs, and are against Christian beliefs. While spiritualism has increased in popularity in the 21st century, we are sometimes so set in our beliefs that we tend to be closed off to other possibilities. Whether you believe séances are real, or simply manifestations of the mind is debatable. But are they dangerous? The answer is both 'yes' and 'no'. If you perform a séance incorrectly, if you don't finish the séance and haven't closed the door that you've opened, or if you're making the séance into a joke, then yes, it can be dangerous. Remember, we have control, we are allowed to tell the spirit that they're not welcome in our lives or homes if that is the case. However, if you do happen to become haunted by any ghosts or demons due to a séance, there are a few signs you can look out for.

PHYSICAL SIGNS OF HAUNTING

Séances can take a toll on us; however, this isn't only limited to mental and emotional exhaustion. Your physical body can take a physical beating while preforming a séance. Not only is adrenaline raging through your body, but your body can easily become tired, especially because a spirit is drawing energy out of you. This can leave you feeling tired and sick for days to come.

If a spirit decides to attach itself to you, there are a few physical signs to look out for. In some beliefs this is called 'ghost sickness'. The most common sign is shortness of breath. This is due to the density of the air, when a spirit is in the room. They draw energy out of a room, making it heavy and dense. This can make it difficult for you to breathe, and you may feel tightness as though something is sitting on your chest.

Another sign, usually related to negative spirits, is nausea. There is no doubt that a negative paranormal attachment may cause you to feel nauseous. Additionally, there are other signs such as headaches and body aches.

But how can you prevent this toll on your body from happening during a séance? A psychic named Craig Hamilton-Parker believes that a great way to defend yourself from becoming sick during and after a séance is through yoga. These physical exercises were designed thousands of years ago not just as a health system, but to prepare the body for the monumental inner changes that happen when a person takes yoga's inner journey to enlightenment. It is said that all individuals who want to partake in mediumship should prepare their body.

PSYCHOLOGICAL SIGNS OF HAUNTING

When someone decides to delve into the art of séance, there can be many troubling questions that arise. This is because the person is often confronted with inner problems that they have to overcome, and this is why performing a séance can be highly emotional. When an individual isn't mentally ready to communicate with spirits, they can become depressed.

Some people who have communicated with spirits have developed mental health issues like depression, exhaustion and hallucinations. It is therefore important that you are mentally prepared to take on the task of a séance. Additionally, you may become deranged, sleep deprived, anxious and depressed if a spirit decides to attach itself to you. Even if you have a positive experience with communicating with the deceased, it can still leave you feeling emotionally overwhelmed. For example, if you happen to contact a passed on loved one, you need to be ready to reopen the wounds from their death. If you are still attached to them, it can be incredibly difficult and emotional to contact them.

You must be able to honestly ask yourself, "Will I be able to communicate with my loved one without emotionally scarring myself?"

SIGNS OF HOUSE HAUNTING

There have been cases where a spirit decides to come home with you, which can be incredibly bad because moving house won't leave the spirit behind. The spirit has attached itself to you, since you've given them a means to live a real life. What are some house haunting signs you should be aware of? While house haunting can be terrifying, before you hear a door creak and think, "Okay, I'm being haunted by a ghost", make sure the noises or odd occurrences aren't because of anything natural, such as a loose door hinge, leaking taps etc. It is easy to let your imagination run wild, so stay calm and open your senses to these signs.

Make sure your thermostat hasn't malfunctioned before concluding that you have an unexplained, possibly ghostly, drop in the temperature. One of the most notable and common signs of a haunting is a drop in temperature. If your house seems to have cold spots, or the room you're in suddenly turns cold, this can be a sign that you're in the presence of a spirit. This, once again, is because they draw out as much energy from their surroundings as possible. Their presence is associated with a sudden or unexplained drop in temperature.

Electrical glitches are another sign of a haunting. Electrical glitches can include anything from ringing phones with no one on the other end of the line to flickering lights, televisions that turn on and off, ringing doorbells and more. Problems with electricity is a classic sign indicating that a ghostly presence is close. Ghosts exist within another dimension and need conduits to make contact, which is why audio and video recording devices have become so well-known as methods of communicating with the spirits.

An unexplained smell is another common sign when dealing with a suspected haunting. One of the most common ways to identify the presence of a ghost is through odour. Ghostly smells will usually be somewhat familiar like perfume, flowers or the distinctive aroma of pipe tobacco. Sometimes, the scents can be less pleasant, like that of sulphur, which has often been connected to hauntings. The smells can manifest and then disappear with no explanation.

While these are just a few signs indicating a possible haunting, it is evident that a séance can be dangerous if done incorrectly.

CHAPTER TWELVE

◆

Communication Devices

There's nothing better than the rush of adrenaline you get when you're trying to contact some invisible presences lurking in your home. Paranormal devices can be terrifying yet exciting and with the rise of technology, there are a number of new devices someone can use to communicate with the deceased.

While we have these new and wonderful gadgets, we also have the techniques that have withstood the test of time. Following on from the analysis of conducting séances and contacting the dead, there are a number of different methods and devices available to contact spirits and create a life changing experience.

OUIJA BOARDS

The Ouija board is the first thing that comes to mind when we talk about paranormal devices. Throughout the centuries, the Ouija board has always been around.

Through the 19th century era of spiritualism to this day and the age of modern mysticism, the Ouija board has been there. When the creators of the Ouija board first started advertising the device in 1891 it became a novelty item in every home. It was widely touted to be able to predict a person's future, and it was promoted just like any board game that might be sold today.

However, as the years have gone by, eerie stories have arisen from the use of these boards. These days, the Ouija board is not so common anymore, outside of mediumship. Crazily enough, the board apparently named itself. The creators held a séance and asked the board what they should name it. The board spelt out 'Ouija' and when asked what it meant; the board spelt out 'Good luck'.

Using a Ouija board is very straightforward. You and the other participants should sit around in a room and eliminate any light and sound. Create a positive atmosphere and pick your medium. Everyone in the room should chant a protection prayer. Next, everyone should lightly place the tip of their fingers on the Planchette and move it around in a few circles to warm up the energy. You should begin by asking simple questions and remain patient. It's easy to use, however, there are rules you need to take note of.

The first rule is that it is not a joke. A session with a Ouija board should be taken extremely seriously, and you should do some research before a session. Yes, it might be an entertaining night for you and your friends, but the consequences can be life damaging if done incorrectly. Furthermore, you should never taunt a ghost, this can make the experience especially intense and even deadly.

You should never ask them dangerous questions, such as when you or someone else is going to die. And take into account that a spirit on the other end of the device can say whatever they wish. But just because they say something, it doesn't necessarily mean that it's true. You should also be careful of malicious spirits who take on the role of a loved one or a friendly ghost in order to gain your trust, so never give yourself over to a spirit.

Another rule would be to never use the board alone, because it needs a lot of energy to use and it can leave you mentally exhausted. Along with that, you should never use a board at your home or in anyone else's home since spirits can attach itself themselves to the real world. You don't want a harmful spirit haunting you in your house.

However, the location you do choose should be darkened and free of background noise. You can use candles to light the board sufficient to see what the planchette is spelling. Don't ever use a Ouija board in a cemetery. Also, it may be a good idea to avoid using a Ouija board if you are experiencing depression, since that kind of low energy draws in malevolent spirits.

Just like a séance, there should be one leader of the group asking the questions, and definitely no jokes. If you aren't the leader of the session, you should keep your fingers on the planchette and remain silent. No one should laugh or ask whether it is 'working', because this negative energy can interfere with the session. Try not to decipher the words as the planchette moves. Your role is to close your eyes and focus your energy on the planchette.

One person should be assigned the task of keeping track of the answers. They should write down the letters/words on a notepad and translate to the group what they think the spirit is saying. Try not to guess what the answers are in the moment. Write down what is happening and do that each time after the planchette stops moving. If you want to take a break, have one person keep their hand on the planchette to stay connected to the energy you've built. Don't leave the planchette on the board, and remove the planchette when you are done with the session. Even if you are just leaving the room for a bit, it's considered bad luck to leave the planchette on the board.

How do you end a session and what if you come into contact with a malevolent spirit? Always end your session with the Ouija board by saying "goodbye", on the board. If a spirit starts communicating with you through the board by counting down or going through the alphabet, immediately end the session by saying, "Goodbye."

This is a common issue with Ouija users who have contacted a malevolent spirit that is trying to leave the board. If a spirit starts communicating with you by making the planchette make a figure 8 or infinity symbol, immediately end the session by saying "Goodbye." This is another way malevolent spirit have revealed themselves.

If you begin to suspect that you are in contact with a malevolent spirit, immediately end the session by putting the planchette on "Goodbye." It also helps to leave the physical space you are in to sever the energy between the group and the spirit. If you speak to a spirit who identifies themselves as 'Zozo', end the session and say "Goodbye" immediately. Zozo has been identified as a malevolent spirit by multiple users.

What should you do if you're having trouble with your board? Just store it away in a little used cupboard and never burn a Ouija board. This can do more damage than simply leaving it untouched in a closet. If you are having problems, store the planchette and board separately.

VOICE RECORDERS

A digital voice recorder is another tool you can use when contacting the dead. You can see this device used in any ghost-hunting movie or television show. Proponents tend to whip out their digital recorder to perform an electronic voice phenomena (EVP) session. This phrase is used for any mysterious voices or sounds caused by ghosts. These small devices are essential for any ghost-hunting enthusiast. But how is it best used?

Before using your recorder for a session, you should make sure that you have sufficient battery power and extra batteries, because spirits tend to drain the energy of a battery. The recorder should be placed on a smooth surface, away from as many obstacles as possible. Make sure that the digital recorder is away from any doors, windows, vents or openings that might cause outside sounds from being recorded. Ensure that the location is quiet by turning off anything that is making a sound, like radios and TVs.

When you have an area that may be active, you have two choices. Either leave your recorder on and unattended, or try to speak with the spirit. Each time, you should start the recording by noting the date and time verbally.

If you decide to leave the recorder running alone, leave the room and mark off the area with tape. Instruct everyone to keep out of the area, but if they must go in there, they should announce their time of entry and departure and make sure they replace the tape when they leave.

To interact with a spirit during a recording session, instruct everyone present to remain as still as possible. Ask questions with at least a 10 second pause in between. Continue on to more specific questions if desired. If anybody makes a noise during the recording, ask them to comment in a normal voice with their name, identifying it was them that made the noise.

You may wish to make a general tour of a location and just randomly sweep for EVP activity. Walk and tour the location while holding the recorder away from your body to reduce movement noise. Always indicate the room you are entering as you are moving through it. Ask questions if desired. If any unexplained noises happen during the recording, verbally note and describe them with the time. When you are finished recording, note the date and time and stop the recording.

NIGHT VISION CAMERAS AND EMF

The next few devices are simple to use and have no real rules to follow. A night vision camera is a must have for every paranormal investigator, or someone who just wishes to see what is really going on in the dark. While the dark can be a scary place for most, especially those who are seeking out spirits, it's important to know what goes on in the late hours of the night. These cameras are great for picking up light anomalies or shadows that we would otherwise miss. Basic night vision recorders don't disrupt electromagnetic fields. Additionally, some of the more high-end cameras, especially made for paranormal investigation, can easily switch to thermal imaging.

Measuring an electromagnetic field (EMF) was an early practice, where mediums walked around rooms with a little TV device. Electricians use this same device to detect harmful radiation in a home. These gadgets are another essential aid to paranormal investigation, and can be used for a ghost-hunt. Ghosts are thought to emit EMF radiation or disturb the existing magnetic fields in a room. But be careful that it isn't your smartphone or any other electronic device that's causing the EMF in a room. However, an anomalous EMF in the middle of a room with no obvious source merits further investigation. This device can easily reveal the 'sweet spots' of a house where you would want to perform further investigation. The more expensive devices can block man-made frequencies through appliances and indicate EMF disturbances with both light and sound alerts.

BINARY RESPONSE DEVICES

The modern-day Ouija Board, is now called a binary response device. This is another important tool if you're wanting to talk to the other side. Investigators can ask suspected spirits yes/no questions, and receive answers through the device. This device allows a spirit to harness the energy in the machine and use it to respond. Different replies are indicated with lights on either side of the device. The gadget features a green and red light to enable yes/no questions (ie: green for YES, red for NO). To obtain answers to slightly more complex inquiries, such as, "which corner of the room are you in?" (ie: red for LEFT, green for RIGHT). You simply need to specify to the spirit how they can respond. In more complex devices there is a YES, NO and MAYBE function along with a full alphabet for longer words. This is much like the old Ouija board.

TAROT CARDS

Another notable mention are Tarot cards. Though, this method isn't necessarily for communicating with the dead, it is a divination tool that psychics use to predict a subject's future. The Tarot is a deck of 78 cards, each with its own imagery, symbolism and story. The 22 Major Arcana cards represent life's karmic and spiritual lessons, and the 56 Minor Arcana cards reflect the trials and tribulations that we experience on a daily basis.

Within the Minor Arcana cards, there are 16 Tarot Court Cards representing 16 different personality characteristics we may choose to express at any given time. The Minor Arcana also includes 40 numbered cards organised into four suits, with ten cards each, representing various day-to-day situations that we encounter. Regrettably, I have stopped using Tarot as a medium because of the possibility of attracting demons.

Every spiritual lesson we come across in our lives can be found in the seventy-eight Tarot cards. When we consult the Tarot, we're shown the exact lessons we need to learn and master to live an inspired life. It's like holding up a mirror to yourself to access your subconscious mind. Tarot allows us to tap into the wisdom and answers that exist in us all.

With all these devices available in the psychic market, it can be easy to be drawn into contacting the dead. But take note that while it can be a very tempting thing to do, it can also become harmful. As discussed in the previous chapter on séance, the very same rules apply to operating these devices, so one should always be serious and cautious. These tools are not toys and should be treated with the utmost respect.

If you and your friends are wanting to entertain each other, you'd be better advised to stick to your normal card games. These tools can cause serious consequences and should not be used unless you're a professional.

CHAPTER THIRTEEN

◆

Psychic Capability

A psychic is a person who claims to use extrasensory perception (ESP) to identify information hidden from the normal senses, particularly involving telepathy or clairvoyance, or who performs acts that are apparently inexplicable by natural laws. Although many people believe in psychic abilities, the scientific consensus is that there is no proof of the existence of such powers and describes the practice as pseudoscience. The word 'psychic' is also used as an adjective to describe such abilities.

Although psychic abilities haven't been proven by scientists, there's no doubt that they're a real thing. People often call it a sixth sense. There have been multiple stories of people with psychic abilities. Many people, when they hear the word 'psychic', think of a creepy old woman sitting in front of a crystal ball, telling your future. But that's not necessarily the case, everyone has access to these abilities in one way or another.

Being psychic doesn't necessarily mean you know what the future is, it can be a rather minor thing. Such as having an insignificant dream that came true once you woke up. It might sound far-fetched, but in reality, most people have some form of psychic ability. The reason why some have stronger psychic abilities than others is because they simply accept it, and have a more open mind. They are therefore more connected to the divine and have more psychic experiences. That's not to say that the average person doesn't have these abilities, everyone does have the ability to have sixth sense. I would like to discuss how someone can strengthen their psychic ability but first, I will describe what the different psychic abilities are.

PSYCHIC ABILITIES

Forget the erroneous notion that psychic readers have to use a crystal ball. A person with psychic capabilities can do so much more than simply look into someone's future, to get the job done. In fact, there are several spiritual and intuitive gifts that are used to provide guidance and answers. There are a few well-known psychic powers you might possess. You may have heard of someone having a sixth sense, but did you know that there are actually six different kinds of 'senses' known as 'Clairs'?

1. Clairvoyance

Clairvoyance is probably one of the most common psychic abilities. This means 'clear seeing'. It refers to the ability to see things in your mind's eye, through visions or dreams. Most people think it is as dramatic as TV. For example, the movie 'Final Destination', is about visions people have of disasters before they come true. However, in real life they may not be as dramatic and many might just brush it off as a strong imagination. Any random vision you have in your mind may come from a divine power, pushing you to do something. The following are some of the experiences I had when I first saw people's lives in my mind, as I touched people, and when I had multiple dreams that came true.

Signs of Clairvoyance

So, what signs might a person show if they have clairvoyant abilities? A true clairvoyant may possess some or all of the following signs: they experience mental images that flash before their eyes; they find it easy to vividly imagine places and people; they see flashes of colour, numbers or symbols; and they feel as if they're watching a movie in their mind.

An easy test of clairvoyance is to notice colours when you close your eyes, which are known as visual psychic flashes. These flashes of colour and light can sometimes be your spirit guides or other members of your spiritual family. You might also see floating orbs or coloured 'blobs' in the air, glowing light around people (their aura), shadows that seem like they are floating in the air, glittering or flashing lights in the air and movement or twinkling lights out of the corner of your eyes.

They daydream easily. Since clairvoyance has to do with seeing, visualisation plays a big part of it. For example, if you're a clairvoyant psychic, it would be easy for you to imagine sipping a Sangria while sitting on a beach on Maui.

They complete visual-spatial tasks easily, like completing a maze in a puzzle book or even perhaps reading a map.

They are drawn to jobs and hobbies that are visually exciting. A clairvoyant psychic might peruse home decorating blogs on a Sunday morning or be drawn to a career as an interior designer or landscaper.

They can envision or make plans in their head, like mapping out a new landscaping idea. They can easily envision how to design a spare room once the antique vanity is painted red.

Someone may also be clairvoyant if they've had any of these experiences: they have always been told that they have a vivid imagination; they had imaginary friends with detailed life stories as a child, and have vivid and/or frequent dreams.

However, you don't need to possess all of these traits to be clairvoyant.

Strengthening Clairvoyance

How does someone strengthen their clairvoyant abilities? Increasing your clairvoyant gifts is easier and probably much more fun than you think! Basically, it's just like learning any other skill. All you need is to practice and be patient, and spend time relaxing, meditating, visualising, and opening your Third Eye Chakra. The following are a few exercises that could help to strengthen clairvoyance:

Exercise 1 - allows you to practice deliberately creating an internal visualisation
- Sit quietly.
- Breathe steadily and close your eyes.

- Imagine a scene in your head. Choose a place in nature, or even another room in your home and put yourself in that scene. Turn your imaginary head to see what's around you.
- Create some action in the scene. Birds, people, anything. You might even have a conversation with someone.
- Then walk away from the scene and imagine coming into the room where you are and sitting down. As though your imagined self and your actual self, have merged.

This should only take a few minutes (or you can make it as long as you like). Practice this exercise daily. Any time you are waiting around, relaxing, or just before bedtime.

Exercise 2 - Receiving Messages
- Sit quietly as before.
- Breathe steadily and close your eyes.
- Don't try to create a scene. Relax and see what arises in your imagination.
- Ask your guides for a message. In your mind, or out loud, say, "Guides, do you have a message for me?"
- Pay attention to the pictures in your mind. If you are prompted by instinct to open your eyes, do so.
- As soon as you feel alone, write down what you saw, heard and felt.

You may not receive a message, but don't be put off, this is an exercise you will need to repeat because it may become your go-to method for 'receiving'.

Exercise 3 - Clairvoyant Peripheral Vision
- Sit quietly, eyes open.
- Breathe steadily.
- Focus on an object placed in front of you. It doesn't matter what it is. A pebble or plant, a pen or a coffee cup will do fine.
- Without moving your focus, become aware of your peripheral vision. In your mind, take note of the objects and furniture around you. If you see shadows or movement, keep focused on the item in front of you.
- Sit for as long as you feel comfortable.
- Make notes on what you saw and felt. Also note any internal vision that took place.

You need to remember to practice because Clairvoyance won't come immediately, and it has to be something you want very much. If possible, practice the above three exercises every day. It doesn't matter too much if you miss a day, or only do one or two of the exercises, but make sure to do all three throughout the week.

Keep a journal of your clairvoyant experiences, and write down any small detail, message, or vision you think is important, or even if it appears unimportant. You never know when that very thing will arise in a conversation. You will be amazed and delighted how often those seemingly random thoughts you recorded are actually connected to a real-life happening, circumstance or conversation. In this way you will train yourself to pay attention to your visions.

2. Clairaudience

Clairaudience is the capability of receiving an intuitive vocal message from the world of spirits or a higher being. Clairaudient people can extend their hearing to transcend the everyday physical world and the known level of awareness, in order to reach the world beyond. Clairaudients are highly intuitive people who are able to listen to a voice other than their own when the spirit world transmits a message to them.

The message might include particular words, names or phrases, unintelligible sounds or music. The voice sometimes sounds extremely different from the voices we normally hear. It may sound as if it's being spoken right next to you, inside your head, or echoing as if from another dimension. It also might sound like one of your loved ones who has passed away. The voice may make itself heard at times of crisis, an emergency, at a crossroads or at another significant time. Clairaudient dreams are also a known phenomenon, where a person may hear the voice of a spirit during sleep.

Clairaudience is much more than simply hearing voices in your head. The main differences between having a mental illness and being clairaudient are very obvious if you know what to look for. While both conditions might include hearing voices within your head, that is where the similarities stop.

Clairaudient mediums can learn to develop a level of control over these voices, and spirit voices tend to not be very constant. Instead, their messages have a tendency to be brief and get straight to the point. They typically engage in a genuine dialogue with the clairaudient person and can answer questions that you have and even provide you with feedback.

Spirit voices in most cases do not prevent functionality or push you towards harmful behaviours. These voices will be more rational, safe, and gentle, and often even more rational than your own voice. In addition, they are usually very compassionate. If you have clairaudience, you will also have the gift of clear speaking. This means that you can channel, share and speak the messages you hear from the spirits to others.

The following are some of the most common signs that you might experience if you are a clairaudient person.

Signs of Clairaudience

If you are clairaudient, it is likely that you find yourself frequently troubleshooting what you say, thinking of replies you would like to give in certain scenarios, and calming yourself down by talking to yourself once stressful events have taken place. In other words, you may talk to yourself. If the replies and solutions you get from doing these things are thoughtful, clear-headed, and calm, then it is likely that the other participant in your conversation is a spirit, and you are hearing them clairaudiently.

You give others good advice. If you find yourself offering great advice to others but have no idea where you got those ideas, then it's possible that those signs came from a spirit. Spirits can speak through you, and when you speak aloud, you might find yourself actually speaking their words. This can also be done through writing.

You always comfort others. If you find yourself comforting others a lot, and especially if you have taken to doing so as a career path, then you might be clairaudient. If you have given your profession and livelihood over to providing others with centred and calming advice, such as by being a counsellor, therapist, nurse, coach, or something similar... this is a strong sign that you maybe clairaudient.

These careers have their main role involved in calming and providing advice to diffuse stress and guide others with thoughtful suggestions. In doing so, it is likely that these words are coming from angels and spirit guides through you, using you as a vessel, without your knowledge. As a result, the advice you give may seem perfectly tailored to what the people around you need at that very moment.

The following are a few exercises that could help to strengthen clairaudient abilities.

- If it is safe to do so, close your eyes and take a few deep breaths.
- Set the intention that you want to increase your psychic hearing.
- Relax your body and allow your hearing to become your dominant sense.
- Gently tune into sounds that you don't normally focus on. What can you hear? Wind soughing through the trees, a full chorus of birds, insects chirruping.

Try this exercise in several locations and let yourself loose to see just how much you can hear. Stretch your psychic hearing in different directions and with different focus. If you've wondered how to develop psychic hearing and rock out to music at the same time, then here is the perfect exercise! It's a lot of fun to perform this exercise with any band that plays heavy instrumentals, and it can also be practiced with classical pieces of music:

- Get your jam on.
- Now focus your attention on just one instrument... oboe, violin, drum. With all instruments playing simultaneously, focus on just one sound until you have isolated it from all the rest.
- With practice, you can then cut one sound away from the others.
- Now choose another instrument and repeat.

3. Clairsentience

The etymology of the word is traced back to the 17th century where *clair,* meaning 'clear' in French, was joined to the word sentient. It is someone who is able to sense or feel things; therefore, clairsentience literally means 'clear sensing' or the ability to clearly sense, perceive or feel things.

On a deeper level, it is the ability to perceive what is usually not perceivable. It means having the ability to feel things as well as one can see them, especially things that are hidden from plain sight. You're not going to find many movies or TV shows based on this skill. It includes intuition, but is much more powerful. Many who seek to enhance their abilities overlook the power of Clairsentience.

A Clairsentient is by their very nature a gentle soul and a great listener. They are not attention seekers as much as they are wallflowers, usually blending into the background, in most social situations and gatherings. They are observers who like to witness rather than to be witnessed. They are quiet but deep souls that don't fit into any other category, because they are in one all of their own.

Everyone wants to see grand visions, but no one talks about the power of feeling. It requires years of practice, skill and a willingness to not only deal with your emotions but everyone else's as well. Clairsentients are naturally great at understanding human behaviour. They understand people without having to know them or spend a great deal of time interacting with them. They can instantly comprehend why someone acts the way they do and understand equally why they can't tolerate it. This allows them to do some of what they do best, bring errant perspectives and people together.

Clairsentients can get to the core of every situation. They find out what lies behind even the deepest of issues that might arise between people. The insights one can achieve when dialoguing directly with the heart are incomparable because we are, by design, deeply emotional creatures who live and breathe through feelings. Therefore, the heart happiness of those a clairsentient advisor engages with, is of vital importance.

What are some of the signs that you could be clairsentient?

Signs of Clairsentience
They feel drained after being in a large group of people. Clairsentients feel energy strongly. So, imagine how

draining it can be to engage with a large group of people for an extended amount of time! Sensing everyone's emotions, moods, and bad days could be the reason they leave work and swim to an island where they can be alone. Clairsentient people NEED to recharge. Quiet time spent alone to rejuvenate is a must.

They have awesome instincts about people, places and situations. Have you ever met someone and just known something about them (and you turned out to be right)? From the sleazy sales guy to the stranger on the street, if you sense people's intentions with no logical explanation, that's a pretty clear indicator that you are clairsentient! Maybe your friends are always coming to you after their dates and asking you what you think about their potential partner. Or maybe you've just known to steer clear of certain people who turned out to be bad news. Either way, that's your clairsentience at work.

They sense energy in the room. Have you ever walked into a room just after an argument and known something had happened, without actually witnessing the fight? Leftover energy is tangible to a clairsentient (which can make crowded places oh-so-draining).

You need a box of Kleenex to watch the news. If you find yourself avoiding the TV news and reading the newspaper, it's a classic sign that clairsentience is one of your psychic abilities. Because it's so easy for empaths to pick up on energy, distressing stories are really difficult to stomach. You can feel the terror of the people who lost everything in the hurricane or feel the anxiety of those impacted by a recent law passed.

You feel emotions (not your own) randomly, and seemingly without cause. If you get waves of emotions for seemingly no reason, don't let your friends convince you it's PMS. You may just be clairsentient! Spirits and energy are constantly around us, and as a clairsentient, you may sense their energies.

Here are a few exercises to help you deepen your clairsentient abilities.

Borrow a friend's friend, or family member. I know that sounds a little weird, but this is SO much fun! Here's what to do:

- Ask a friend to show you a picture of someone they know very well, but you've never met or heard much about.
- Once they show you the picture, focus on the person's eyes, and feel how they were feeling when the picture was taken. Were they happy? Sad? Anxious? Would you trust this person?
- When you're done, ask your friend for feedback! Did you sense that the person was happy, only to find out that the picture was taken right after their NFL team won the Super bowl? Or did you sense they were trustworthy to find out that they helped your friend through a really difficult time?

Sense the energy from a personal object. Did you know that your favourite sweater, treasured family locket, and well-loved childhood stuffed animal have all absorbed some of your energy? Our energy transfers to the things we own — and the more we use/wear/treasure the object, the more energy there is.

One of the most fabulous ways to develop clairsentience is to practice psychometry. Psychometry means reading the energy off an object and here's how to do it:

- Invite your friend over. Ask them to bring over a family heirloom or piece of jewelry. (Tip: jewelry works great because metal can hold energy like forever!) Make sure the object is from someone that you have never met.
- Rub your hands together and take some deep breaths.
- Hold the object for a few minutes. Try to sense what kind of energy it's giving off. Is it positive or negative?
- Now, sense the energy of the person who owns or owned the object. Are/were they happy? Humorous? Depressed?

4. Clairalience

This one is strange, but not so uncommon. This is the ability to psychically smell. Scent has an incredible way of evoking memory and emotion. Whether that's the scent of your grandma's chocolate chip cookies, a fresh cut lawn, or your grandfather's cologne. Certain scents carry certain levels of meaning. The way another person smells can be attractive or off-putting. Smell is a powerful sense and it's not just limited to the physical realm. Clairalience, or clear smelling, occurs to both psychic and non-psychic people. It's not something that you can consciously initiate. Instead, it's something that most often occurs as a sign or guidance from your spirit team. It's a wonderful gift to receive and to develop. Clairalience is a powerful psychic tool. Those with a developed sense of clairalience smell things that are too subtle for others. And, more often than not, these particular smells contain messages or other divine information.

When you catch the signature scent of your loved one in Spirit or a scent that simply reminds you of time you spent with that person, it could be a sign that his or her spirit is near. This could be cologne or perfume, their brand of smoke (if they were a smoker), or even the smell of cookies, or freshly baked bread if they loved to bake. When you experience the signature scent of a loved one in Spirit, this is often a sign their spirit is with you, wanting you to know they're nearby. Even if you find yourself smelling scents that remind you of people you had a difficult past with, it could be their spirit attempting to make things right by causing you to remember and process your feelings.

You can even smell when negative energy is around you; usually in the odour of sulphur, rotting meat or sewage. This is a sign of demonic energy or negative energy. What are some of the signs that you may be clairalient?

Signs of Clairalience

The simplest sign that you're clairalient is smelling a scent that has an unknown source, even though it might come and go quickly. Maybe you smell a lovely perfume. If there isn't any particular source it's coming from, then that's a sign you have the ability to smell the spirit dimension. But there are a few other signs as well.

You may be able to recall difficult-to-access memories, since a smell can bring back a person or situation that you'd forgotten about on a conscious level. It's as simple as smelling your mother's perfume then feeling your mother's presence, to something as complex as a smell reminding you of an obscure childhood memory at school that you perhaps repressed.

It's possible for a smell to evoke a psychic impression in order to get a feeling about someone. So, being able to 'read' other people is a sure sign of clairalience. Smells that may be so subtle yet can tell you if a person is attracted to you or not, or if someone is very ill are good examples. It's also possible to smell if someone is uncomfortable, annoyed, lying, or scared.

Sensing danger is another attribute of a Clairalient. On a physical level, people can smell rotten food which warns us not to eat it, or they can smell gas and know there is a leak. On a psychic level however, it is possible to smell danger. You may not be able to verbally define it at that moment, but clairalience is telling you that something isn't right.

The following are a few exercises you can do to develop and strengthen this ability.

First, you should smell everything, including roses or the fruits and vegetables at the supermarket (it's also a good way to tell if they're ripe and ready to eat). Smell your pets and your kids, and just allow yourself to become aware of the smells around you. Once you smell a certain scent, notice how the smell makes you feel emotionally and psychically. This meditation exercise works best in a small group setting or with a partner.

- Sitting in a circle or across from your partner, go into a meditative state with the intention of opening up and developing your intuitive sense of smell.
- First, pull your conscious awareness inside yourself and settle your energy. Then, allow your conscious awareness to extend out to another person in the circle, or to your partner. Imagine yourself breathing in the energy around them.
- As you breathe in their energy, ask to receive smell impressions. What do you smell and connect with? If you also receive information in the form of taste, sounds, images or colours, that's okay. If so, what does that colour smell like? What does the taste smell like?
- Record your impressions, then withdraw your conscious awareness from their energy field and allow yourself a deep, cleansing breath. Then move on to the next person in the circle until you're done.
- Share your impressions, because you might find (as I did when I repeated this exercise in a development circle) that several people in the circle get the same smells, colours and impressions for a particular person. This under-rated intuitive sense can really be remarkable.

5. Clairgustance

This psychic ability is similar to clairalience, except it involves taste. Clairgustance or 'clear taste' is probably the most unusual of all the psychic phenomena. It is a form of extra-sensory perception (ESP) that allows the gifted person to taste a substance associated with someone or something from the past, present or future.

Psychics and mediums with the psychic ability of 'clear taste' basically experience a variety of taste sensations, without actually placing anything on their tongue, or into their mouth. Clairgustance therefore enables us to receive messages from the spiritual realm by 'tasting' the essence of various substances in the form of 'non-physical flavours' or taste sensations. The effect is ultimately similar to our normal sense of taste, but the items tasted are not physically present.

What could the purpose of such an odd psychic sense possibly be? Well, believe it or not, it does come in handy! Psychics who work in law-enforcement or forensics, for example, benefit greatly from their ability to become aware of the taste of chemicals, drugs or blood. It often provides clues to how a victim died, or how the crime was committed.

Some medical intuitivists can taste certain foods a person may need for their health, such as the taste of orange juice for someone who lacks Vitamin C. The taste of certain medicinal substances could also indicate a possible cause of illness, or what kind of treatment to seek. It is also very handy in some situations if you can 'taste' something that is harmful or dangerous. This enables an ability to receive the necessary information about what or where the substance was, without having to physically expose yourself to it.

Mediums rely on clairgustance most often to identify the source or reason for a message, or to communicate with the consciousness of a loved one who has passed. In this case the various tastes are directly associated with those they are communicating with. Nothing is more validating than an accurate description of your granny's home-baked cinnamon biscuits, made from her secret recipe, or your uncle's favourite ketchup, with which he always smothered his food at family celebrations!

But this gift of taste is not only applicable to the deceased, or non-physical entities. Psychics also experience tastes that are linked to the living. What are signs that you may have this psychic ability?

Signs of Clairgustance

A sign of clairgustance is having a taste in your mouth with no idea where it came from because you haven't eaten anything. The taste can be pleasant or unpleasant. Unpleasant tastes usually occur to protect us from danger, or foods that may contain poison. It doesn't have to be because you simply forgot to brush your teeth!

Another sign is having a love for food, or perhaps you're a chef. If you really enjoy all the wonderful tastes that come with food, it might be another sign of this psychic ability.

Maybe you taste something, and have no idea where it came from, but it reminds you of an experience you've had in your past. Like all psychic abilities, they usually come with no rational sources. They simply trigger something inside of ourselves. The following is an exercise that you can practice to strengthen clairgustance skills, and is about being conscious of your food:

- Find a spot to eat the food, with minimum distractions.
- Take a bite of the food and chew slowly. Think about every taste of it. Is it spicy? Sweet? Sour? Or is it the perfect mix?

- With every different food on your plate, be aware of how each one tastes. Is there anything you can take away from it? Does the food provoke negative or positive feelings in you? How does your body feel when you eat this good?
- This exercise may also help you to improve your diet.

6. Claircognisance

This psychic ability is all about intuitively 'knowing' something from nowhere. Do you ever feel like you 'just know' things? Do you have especially good insights in the shower or while you're driving? Have you ever known who's on the other end of the line the instant the phone rings? These are instances of claircognisance, or clear knowing, that many of us feel, but often discount because they're so ordinary.

Of all the forms of knowing, ie: clairvoyance, clairsentience, etc., claircognisance is arguably the least sexy and hardest to discern. But some psychics argue that experiencing clear knowing is a sign that you've intuitively 'arrived'. While claircognisance might not be as fun as clairvoyance or even clairaudience, I have to agree that now that I've cultivated this skill, it's great to just ... know. Clear knowing cuts out the middleman of your five senses, and so it takes quite a bit of trust to work with and to recognise.

There are many ways you could receive divine information. It could also be in the form of synchronicities, which is what psychics like to call a coincidence, except it's not a coincidence at all because it was meant to happen. What are the signs you may have this psychic ability?

Signs of Claircognisance

You are a 'thinker'. Those of us with busy, often logical, minds frequently have flashes of insight, especially about a problem or puzzle in our lives. However, these flashes can be so common that we don't recognise them as the instant psychic downloads they are.

You interrupt people. No, it's not just bad manners! Claircognisant individuals often know what another person is going to say in a conversation, so they respond before the person can even get a full sentence out. If you can often complete other people's sentences, you may have this ability.

You have powerful, specific hunches. Vague intuition is different from the sense of certainty you may get when someone is lying, doing something sketchy, or presenting a false self. If you can often sass out when people are being dishonest, even when everyone else is fooled, you are likely claircognisant.

You are the go-to problem solver for your tribe. If you are the one everyone comes to with a problem, from crosswords to personal dilemmas to reinventing the wheel, you may be claircognisant. The following are a few exercises you can practice to further develop your claircognisant ability.

Exercise 1: Claircognisance Visualisation Exercise:
- Start by pulling out your journal and pen.
- Write about how your life will be when your claircognisance is fine-tuned and increased.

- Describe a day in your life where you 'know' that you should do something, and it has a positive impact on your life. For example, you 'know' you need to stop by at Starbucks on the way home, where you happen to run into your old boss who offers you a dream job in her new start-up!

- Visualise how your inner 'knowing' will make you feel and how that would impact on your day-to-day life.

- Then, set your journal aside, and meditate on the day you just described. Visualise everything in detail.

- Put yourself in the moment and imagine how your body feels when you are experiencing a claircognisant episode.

- Meditate on the specifics of your day and the increased claircognisance.

Exercise 2: Automatic writing is another exercise you can try:

- Grab a pen and pull out your notebook. Before you start writing, ask your Higher Self a question.

- Then write whatever comes to you. Seriously, whatever! Even if it seems like gibberish. Let your pen flow!

- The first few times you do this exercise it may seem totally ludicrous. But those times will clear out your subconscious and make room for the good stuff. And in no time at all, your page will start to be filled with things that make sense. In other words, you'll be receiving clear claircognisant messages and your inner knowing will become much stronger!

These are the main psychic abilities. However, there are many more other skills you can have since everyone is unique, and everyone's abilities are unique. Psychic abilities can be experienced in many forms. It's important to trust your intuition when it comes down to it, because everyone has the ability to be psychic, and it's all about awakening those skills from within.

Another way you may possess psychic ability is through 'precognition', which is having dreams that come true. 'Remote viewing' is another ability, which links in to clairvoyance, as an ability to view things or places in your own mind, which are real, without actually being there in physical form.

Psychic abilities are beautiful to have and are truly a gift since they lead you down the path you're meant to be on. However, it's important to be cautious and careful when it comes to opening up yourself to the spirit world, because it can introduce negative consequences that scar you for life. In the next chapter I'll be talking about how some of these experiences have scarred and traumatised me throughout my life, and how we can deal with them and move forward.

CHAPTER FOURTEEN

◆

Life After Death

You will understand by now, and as discussed a number of times throughout this book so far, there is life after death. Even if one is sceptical, there are many signs and stories that prove otherwise. With all these experiences that people talk about, whether psychic or paranormal, it still might not be enough for many to believe. This chapter introduces the related concepts of near-death experiences and astral travel. These situations and knowledge haven't just come from thin air. These are real experiences that happen to real people.

A good place to begin is with the very touchy subject of death. Near-death experiences prove that there is a life after death. It's not all just blackness. We are merely a soul living a human experience for a time. Once that experience is over, we go somewhere new, in order to grow our soul further.

What is a near-death experience (NDE)? Near-death experiences are a common enough concept that they have entered into our everyday language. Phrases like "my whole life flashed before my eyes," and "go to the light" come from decades of research into these strange, seemingly supernatural experiences that some people have when they're at the brink of death. But are NDE's proof of life after death?

Dr. Raymond Moody coined the term "near-death experience" in his 1975 book, "Life After Life".[1]

Many credit Moody's work with bringing the concept of the near-death experience to the public's attention, but similar reports of such experiences have occurred throughout history. Plato's 'Republic', written in 360 B.C.E., contains the tale of a soldier named 'Er' who had an NDE after nearly being killed in battle. Er described his soul leaving his body, being judged along with other souls and seeing heaven.

A near-death experience is any experience in which someone close to death, or suffering from some trauma or disease that might lead to death, perceives events that seem to be impossible, unusual or supernatural.

While there are many questions about NDEs, one thing is certain, they do occur. Thousands of people have actually perceived similar sensations while close to death. The debate is over whether or not they actually experienced what they perceived.

TRAITS OF THE NDE

Most NDEs share certain common traits, but not all NDEs exhibit every trait and some NDEs don't follow a pattern at all. However, 'typical' NDEs share a number of common traits:

- Intense, pure bright light. Sometimes this intense, but not painful light fills the room. In other cases, the subject sees a light that they feel represents either heaven or God.

- Out-of-body experiences (OBE), are said to have occurred when the subject feels that they have left their body. They can look down and see their body, often describing the sight of doctors working on them. In some cases, the subject's 'spirit' then flies out of the room, into the sky and sometimes into space.

- Depending on the subject's religious beliefs and the nature of the experience, they enter into another realm or dimension and may perceive this realm as heaven or, in some rare cases, as hell.

- During the OBE, the subject may encounter spirit beings, 'beings of light', or other representations of spiritual entities. They may perceive these as deceased loved ones, angels, saints or God.

- Many NDE subjects find themselves in a tunnel with a light at its end, and may even encounter spirit beings as they pass through the tunnel.

- Before the NDE ends, many subjects report some form of communication with a spirit being. This is often expressed as a hearing a 'strong male voice' telling them that it is not their time and to go back into their body. Some subjects report being told to choose between going into the light or returning to their earthly body. Others feel they have been compelled to return to their body by a voiceless command, possibly coming from God.

- Another NDE trait is called 'the panoramic life review'. The PLR subject sees his entire life in a flashback. These observations can be very detailed or very brief. The subject may also perceive some form of judgment by nearby spirit entities.

Near-death experiences and out-of-body experiences are sometimes grouped together, but there are a number of key differences. An OBE can be a component of an NDE, but some people experience OBEs in circumstances that have nothing to do with death or dying. They may still have spiritual elements or feelings of calm. OBEs can happen spontaneously, or can be induced by drugs or meditation.

A statistical analysis of more than one hundred NDE subjects revealed that prior religious belief and prior knowledge of NDEs did not have an appreciable effect on the likelihood of having an NDE.

Other research has focused on the effect an NDE has on the subject's life. Kenneth Ring, one of the most prolific researchers and authors of NDE studies, reported a large number of subjects who gained self-confidence and became more extroverted after an experience. [2] One of Ring's studies quantified changes in subjects' attitudes toward life. These generally included a sense of purpose in life, an appreciation of life, and increase in compassion, patience and understanding and an overall feeling of personal strength.

A small percentage of subjects reported feelings of fear, depression and a focus on death. Ring also found that NDE subjects tended to feel a heightened sense of religious feeling and a belief in the spiritual world. However, he noted that this did not necessarily translate into an increase in church attendance, as it was more of an internal, personal increase in religious and spiritual feelings.

Finally, people who go through NDEs often find that they no longer fear death, and feel that a positive experience will be awaiting them when they actually die.

Next, we examine the spiritual and supernatural theories that attempt to explain near-death experiences. Theories explaining near-death experiences fall into two basic categories: scientific explanations (including medical, physiological and psychological) and supernatural explanations (including spiritual and religious).

Of course, because an acceptance of supernatural explanations is based on faith, spiritual and cultural background, these explanations can be neither proven nor disproven.

The most basic supernatural explanation is that someone who goes through an NDE is actually experiencing and remembering things that happen to their disembodied consciousness. When they are near death, their soul leaves their body and they begin to perceive things that they normally cannot. The soul passes through the border between our world and the afterlife, usually represented by a tunnel with a light at the end.

While on this journey, the soul encounters other spiritual entities (souls), and may even encounter a divine entity, which many subjects perceive as God. They are offered a glimpse into another realm of being, often thought to be 'heaven', but they are then pulled back, or choose to return to their earthly body.

I can say in the course of my life, I have had a few close calls that could have potentially changed my life or ended it. I've never had the classic near-death experience or out of body moment, when one's spirit floats away from one's body, or hovers in a state of heightened awareness from the ceiling or some higher plane. However, there have been many reported cases of near-death experiences with some saying they were greeted by God in heaven and told that it was not yet their time to cross over into the other realm.

I believe their stories are true, although every human experience will differ. The end result however, is the same as it simply isn't that soul's time to leave the earth so they must return to their physical body. Whether it was God or the angels who told them this and sent them back, or whether they just made it back into their body on their own accord, seems irrelevant.

A similar concept is 'astral travel', also known as astral projection. It is a term used in esotericism to describe an intentional out of body experience that assumes the existence of a soul or consciousness called an astral body, that is separate from the physical body and capable of travelling outside itself through the universe.

Essentially, the OBE begins with an experience of leaving the body and consciously observing it from a detached perspective. With practice and lucidity, awareness can be directed to locations or activities like flight... yes, flight! If you've had flying dreams, literally flying, or being in the sky, you've had OBEs. Some say that we have regular OBEs during sleep, often hovering a few inches over our physical bodies.

Neuroscientists are puzzled that while the experience is no longer dismissed out of hand by medical professionals, science holds the view that OBEs involve neurological or brain dysfunction. After his own experience, Dr. Raymond Moody MD became interested in near death OBEs. For decades he interviewed hundreds of events and collected data, defining common qualities of OBEs. Moody identified nine common elements of a near-death OBE, with some experiencing all of the elements in their event, while others, only two or three.

BENEFITS OF OBE

The tantric mastered lucid OBE and dream states to overcome the fear of death by learning that we are not our 'bodies'. They also discovered that the physical body can experience deep healing during OBEs, and that the mind can be tough on the body. Rather than losing time to practice meditation during sleep, yogis continued working through the night while the body rested.

Some athletes learn lucid dreaming to practice and visualise their game. By working in a dream or out-of-body, not only do they visualise, they have a 'felt sense' of their practice and can actually acquire the muscle memory for winning habits. Others benefit from the opportunity to explore past lives as well as accelerated personal development.

Although this kind of travel is intentional, not everybody knows or becomes aware that they have astral projected, which is a similar experience to a near death experience. Have you ever woken up because you feel like you're falling through the bed? This is your soul returning to your body after an out of body experience. Our souls are actually travelling whilst we sleep, which allows us to dream and this is called astral projection. While you are astral travelling, you remain in your physical body and process the projection of 'consciousness' into visual scenes with the effect of feeling as if you are there.

Would you like to know how to astral project? I will share some beginners' tips with you.

First, focus on your breathing, control it at all times, breathing deeply in and out until you start to feel like your mind is emptying. There should be nothing on your mind except the sound of your breathing. At some point you will start to feel strange, numb or even disconnected. If this isn't happening you need to continue your breathing and relax as much as you can. This takes a lot of practice.

After about fifteen minutes you'll experience a heavy feeling, as if a heavy blanket was placed over your body, you may even lose the awareness of your physical body, but just let this happen without fearing it.

Second, comes the vibrational stage where you start to shift your consciousness into a different vibrational frequency in order to project. For first timers it may seem all a little weird. Then let the vibrations pass over you, staying focused and don't panic. Once this has settled in and you're at the vibration stage, you can start to exercise your willpower, and the direction you take is up to you.

Third, visualise yourself moving, without physically moving, like practicing 'telekinesis'. This is where the projection comes into play; you now need to lift yourself in your new relaxed state out of your physical body. Some say to imagine your hand opening and closing without it actually moving and just focus on the feeling until you almost see your hand move. When you have found what works for you and you've focused on the visual aspect, exercise all your willpower and push out of your body.

Finally, you need to rise up from your body. You will naturally be drawn strongly back to your body for the first few attempts. However, it does improve with an ample amount of practice, when you have the time, of course. It is healthy to maintain a balance between the physical world and the astral, so I advise the sceptics as well as non-sceptics to give it a go.

The Rope Method

Another method of projecting oneself out of the body is called the Robert Bruce method, or 'the rope method'. The 'rope technique' is initiated by attaining a deep meditative state. This is no easy task and will likely take significant amounts of practice to achieve before being able to go further. Once this state is attained, we are told to picture a rope hanging above our heads. Then we must concentrate and visualise reaching out of our body with our astral arms, using our spiritual instead of our physical body, grip the rope, and continuously climb upward. We should carry on climbing until we feel as though we're climbing out of our own body.

During this visualisation, focus should be placed on the pressure exerted by the rope on our astral hands. This helps to transfer our sensory awareness from the physical to the spiritual. Eventually, the sensation of increasingly intense vibrations will be experienced. Focusing on the vibrations is said to be the final step before the entire astral body becomes disconnected from the physical self. We should then be able to pull our astral selves free of the physical body using the rope and be able visit alternate planes of existence.

Lucid Dreaming

There's a lot of speculation that lucid dreaming and astral projection are the same, but there are distinct differences. A lucid dream occurs when the dreamer is aware that they are dreaming. During a lucid dream, the dreamer may gain some amount of control over the dream characters, narrative and environment. However, this is not actually necessary for a dream to be described as lucid. But how is it different to astral projection?

When you experience a lucid dream, you are actually asleep, and the experience is therefore not real. You can choose where your dream begins, where it ends and who accompanies you on the journey. Your consciousness remains merged with your physical body, as it would in a normal dream and in everyday life. You can manipulate the environment to appear whenever you choose.

Lucid dreaming is different from astral projection because to astral project you cannot be asleep. The point of projection comes just before the physical body falls asleep. You must retain consciousness. For this reason, the experience is real. You can't choose where you start or finish your astral projection. Your experience begins and ends wherever you began. Your body remains in the same place while your consciousness leaves your physical body and travels on the astral plane. You cannot control the beings on the astral plane, but like in the physical world, you can manipulate conversations and interactions to a degree. You can't however, change the environment to what you want to see since this realm exists whether you're visiting or not. When you have finished projecting, your consciousness merges with your physical body.

Understanding the difference between astral projection and lucid dreaming will help you cultivate the desired experience, both of which are very exciting. When astral projecting you separate your consciousness from your physical assets, and you will instantly know that you are NOT dreaming because you will sense that you are fully conscious. When lucid dreaming you will know you are not astral projecting because you will be in complete control of your environment, the characters, trees, sky and animals.

Parallel Universe

Another important 'life after death' topic that can easily become confusing is parallel universes. This is not so much a spirit world, though it can be mistaken as one. A parallel universe, also known as a parallel dimension, alternate universe or alternate reality is a hypothetical self-contained plane of existence or co-existence with others. I once saw this family dressed in clothes from the eighteen-hundreds standing at a train station. Initially I thought they were spirits but now I believe that they were actually there in their own time, and they were merely present in a parallel universe.

Have you ever been driving or walking along and thought to yourself, "there could be a dinosaur drinking from that river right there, right now?" How do you think mediums, psychics, gypsies can tell your past, present, and future? The answer is because all three have already happened in parallel worlds. Time is not linear as every moment is happening at once. However, our minds are just 'tuned-in' to the frequency of one moment. Otherwise, if everything happened at once, living would be impossible.

The gift of tuning into and seeking an insight into the past, present, or future is often seen as magic. This is mostly forbidden and falls under the category of sin, which is why I stopped doing readings for people after my brush with the demonic world. This is to ensure I don't somehow attract another negative being by opening myself up to the spirit world.

Dimensions

Did you know that there is more than one universe, that are sometimes called dimensions? Although I cannot tell you how many dimensions there are, some people think there is only one, while others think the number can be endless, While I'm only positive about three in past, present and the future dimension, I have a hunch that there may be five or more.

What I've come to know is that there are five universes, with the first being infinite universes. There are also bubble universes, daughter universes, mathematical universes and of course parallel universes. Going way back to the idea that space-time is flat the number of possible particle configurations in multiple universes would be limited to $10^{10^{122}}$ according to what I have researched in the past distinct possibilities. With an infinite number of cosmic patches, the particle arrangements within them have to repeat infinitely many times over. So that then means there are infinitely many parallel universes.

The cosmic patches are the same as ours containing someone exactly like you, as well as patches that differ by just one or two particle positions. This means that everything is the same except for certain minor details. There is a theory known as the 'Mandela Effect', which refers to a widely shared but false memory, which happened due to a parallel universe crossing over with our plane.

The 'Mandela Effect' came about when thousands of people believed that Nelson Mandela had died in the 1980s, but he actually later became president of South Africa and died in 2013. The false memory however, was collectively shared. There are many other memories that we all seem to have, that never actually happened. For example, everyone remembers the monopoly man, from the monopoly board game who wears a monocle (one eyeglass). However, it turns out that in fact, he doesn't and has never had one, yet somehow most people believe it to be true.

Not everyone will agree with the theory of parallel universes, and I shall leave it up to you. However, some day you might come across what you think are spirits that are actually just living in our past or future, or you might even see an older or younger version of yourself, as portrayed in 'the Chronicles of Narnia'. Could that be possible?

Because of the wide range of stories involving all these events, and the similarities that occur between different individuals, it's evident to me that these phenomena aren't made up. There is something more to it. While researchers are still trying to discover the meaning of these events, we do know that past lives are real. Whether it's in our mind or not, it is true that we go somewhere beyond the physical, once our bodies die. We aren't only limited to one life because there are many dimensions, which is good news for us, since we don't need to be afraid of death.

CHAPTER FIFTEEN

◆

Manifestation

In chapter ten, the topic of 'how to keep your soul safe', was introduced and we discussed how negative energy can attract negative energy. But this concept needs examination in more depth, and especially what is known as the law of attraction, or manifestation.

Manifestation is the transmutation of thought into its physical equivalent. It's the process of taking an idea, a dream, a goal or a vision and taking the necessary action steps to make it a reality. Anything you can daydream about, can be created in your life.

> "Imagination is everything, it is the preview of life's coming attractions"
> - *Albert Einstein*

The Latin root of 'manifestation' is 'manifestare' which means 'to make public'. Quite literally, when you manifest, you make your goals and dreams public. You pull them out of your mind and into the physical world. This requires focused determination and faith.

When you hear someone talking about manifestation, they are usually talking about 'intentional manifestation'. But in reality, we unintentionally manifest all day long. As analytical beings, our minds are constantly overthinking our current reality. This causes us to unintentionally manifest more of what we already have, or don't have, into our future. Intentional manifesting requires us to shift our dominating thought patterns to support the reality we want to create, whether or not we are currently living that reality.

Although this can sound quite wishy-washy and religious, it actually holds a lot of scientific relevance. If we really think about it, it's simple. Everything is made from atoms, which are structured in different ways. Our human body, plants, food, objects and virtually everything else consists of atoms. These atoms are placed into a structure called a lattice, which moves. As these lattices of atoms come together to form something, they move, and it is this movement of atoms that creates an energy.

This is why crystals have a certain energy, the movement of their atoms are creating this energy. As humans, we are giving off energy all the time. However, our energy isn't so straightforward, since it can be affected by our thoughts and emotions. And while we're always around other people and other objects, our energy field, otherwise known as an 'aura', is picking up and absorbing that energy.

Interestingly, even our thoughts have an energy. An experiment on this topic concerned two different glasses of water. The first glass was told beautiful things and spoken to kindly, while the other glass was spoken to negatively. Once the water of the two different glasses were frozen, there was an interesting result. The water that was spoken to positively formed beautiful structures, while the water that was spoken to negatively looked mushy and chaotic, and didn't have the same beautiful patterns.

The experiment concluded that our words, intentions and thoughts can greatly affect ourselves and others. However, in thinking about the results, how does this affect our bodies, which also consist mostly of water?

What do you think happens when you continuously tell yourself that you are ugly, depressed, unworthy, unlovable, a failure, etc.? You're going to attract exactly that into your life! If you tell yourself that you are ugly, you're going to attract more ugliness into your life. If you tell yourself that you are poor, you attract more poverty into your life. But on the other hand, by telling yourself that you're beautiful, you will become beautiful.

What does this have to do with demons? Well, there are different planes of consciousness, and humans generally fall into the 'neutral' plane. This means that their energy is neither extremely high, nor extremely low. Human beings in fact range between these extremes and can attract both positive and negative energy.

However, because humans aren't always one hundred percent happy, harmonious and in peace, they will never be on the high energy plane, where angels live. On the other hand, humans aren't always one hundred percent sad, angry, depressed or harbour feelings of guilt. Therefore, they won't normally fall into that plane, where demons live.

Humans who are more often sad, angry, guilty, etc. than happy, will have lower energy and demons like this. Indeed, demons can only exist in this low energy plane, which is why there aren't any demons in heaven. Therefore, if you're in a low vibrational energy state, it is much easier for demons to attach and possess you or oppress you.

Returning to manifesting, we are always manifesting and attracting things into our lives. Like gravity, manifestation doesn't disappear, it is always there, whether or not you're aware of it. That's why it's called a universal law.

We often don't realise what we are thinking and our brains are an organ we can't switch off. And it's crazy to try and control each and every one of your thoughts. However, it's not impossible to change our thinking patterns through practice. If you look at yourself every morning in the mirror and think, "I'm so ugly," it's natural for this self-concept to become habitual. And, once this habit is formed, it'll be your natural thought every time you look in the mirror. However, if you practice looking in the mirror and tell yourself, "I'm a beautiful person", it will also will become habit, and it will have an effect on your persona.

You can use this technique with anything. Maybe you want more money, to be happier, or to feel more attractive. The more positive we are, the more abundance we attract into our lives. Isn't it crazy knowing that you can have absolutely anything that you want? But how chaotic would life be if you instantly got something you thought about. What if you thought of an elephant, and just like that... an elephant appeared in your bedroom? Life obviously can't and doesn't work that way, which is why manifestation takes time and practice, and the more often it's done the better.

The 'Law of Attraction' is an essential part of the manifestation process because if you know how to use it to your benefit, it is the very force that will bring your desires into your life. Most goals, dreams and desires all exist in a high vibration state. By learning to cultivate a high vibration state, you will become a magnet to a high vibration reality and your high vibration goals. If your goal is to experience a life of happiness, love, joy, fulfillment and abundance, then you must first generate those emotions in your body's vibration.

Like attracts like, otherwise known as the 'Law of Attraction' which contends that an elevated emotional state will inevitably attract the people, opportunities and situations aligned with your goals, and from there it's up to you to take action. There are thousands of people who have used the technique to live their dream life. The following are examples of known and not so well-known people who have harnessed the power of manifestation.

The actor, Jim Carrey, used manifestation to make money from acting, and his big check is a well-known story among struggling actors in Hollywood. This story took place years before Jim Carrey became the celebrated actor he is today. He was a virtually unknown young comic in Los Angeles, in 1990. Dreaming about his future, Jim wrote himself a check for $10 million dollars for 'acting services'. Even though he was poor at the time, he believed in the power of what he wrote and dated the check for Thanksgiving of 1995. He placed the check inside his wallet and left it there. When Thanksgiving '95 rolled around, Jim Carrey was worth much more than what he had manifested, with his fee for each film being a whopping $20 million.

Another great example is Arnold Schwarzenegger's story.

"When I was very young, I visualised myself being and having what it was that I wanted. Mentally, I never had any doubts about it. The mind is really so incredible. Before I won my first Mr. Universe title, I walked around the tournament like I owned it. The title was already mine. I had won it so many times in my mind that there was no doubt I would win it. Then when I moved on to the movies, the same thing. I visualised myself being a famous actor and earning big money. I could feel and taste the success. I just knew it would all happen, and it did."

Another experience comes from Denise Duffield-Thomas, coach and motivational speaker.

"The last year and a half has been the luckiest and most amazing time of my life, so far. It also coincided with me experimenting with the Law of Attraction and other well-known personal development principles. In one year, I achieved some almost unbelievable goals and manifested almost £500,000 (almost half a million) worth of free things and activities that directly related to those goals."

And a woman named Sylvia was also successful with manifestation.

"I was in a down-time of my life, working a hard door-to-door sales job. It was a hot summer day, and I pulled my car up in front of a beautiful home sitting on the edge of a picture-perfect lake to eat a peanut butter sandwich that I had made for my lunch. I sat and thanked god for the beauty around me and cried about my situation. I asked why I was living in a cheap apartment in town, when all these people are living in beautiful homes on this beautiful lake. Was I loved so much less than they were? I imagined myself floating on the lake in the boat that was attached to the dock across the street from the pretty house.

A couple of days later I was sitting in bed reading the for-sale ads in the newspaper and there in bold print was: FREE HOUSE. I said to my husband there is something we can afford. So, I called the number, and it wasn't exactly true, it was: come and take over my loan, but you need no money down to buy it. I will quick claim it to you. I have to leave the area, and the house can be yours.

So, we went to see it. It was the exact house I had been sitting in front of a couple of days earlier, pleading for a house like it! I had visualised myself in it, asked for it, and as always thanked for what I already had as it was much. And, it was given to me!"

So, how can you practice manifestation to get the life of your dreams? There are three basic steps for manifesting desires into reality. Use these steps literally and consistently and you will reconnect to your intuitive guidance, witness tangible results and manifest any goal, desire or dream into reality.

HOW TO USE MANIFESTATION

The first step in the manifestation process is to establish your purpose. Making clear purposeful goals creates a strong foundation for the rest of the process. Not taking time to connect your goals and dreams to their larger impact, can lead to burn-out and distraction. By making goals bigger than yourself, you invite in the power of community, the laws of the universe and the power of your mind, to keep you going through the inevitable challenges your journey will encounter. Take some time to meditate and reflect upon your goals. What is the underlying motivation behind them? For example, if you're hoping to manifest a raise in your salaried job, ask yourself:

- Why do I want a raise at work?
- Who else will benefit when I have a higher salary?
- How will I make the world a better place if I get paid more?

You will use these answers to help motivate you when the going gets tough along your journey.

The second step in the manifestation process is to create systems that will keep your vibration high, lift your spirits and keep your faith strong. Create a definite plan for the attainment of your desires and take immediate action on that plan. The plan might change along the way, and that's okay too, so be prepared to modify and diversify your goals. In addition to clear action steps, your success system should include daily mindset or personal development work. As already stated, the Law of Attraction is a catalyst for manifestation. It can either speed up or slow down the physical attainment of your goal depending on one thing, which is YOU.

Therefore, your energy towards your goal will determine how fast it comes to you. Creating success systems includes:

- Gathering community support
- Investing in continued education

- Consistently utilising mental, spiritual, and emotional practices

All of these processes will help empower you to maintain focused determination on your goals. Another way to keep your spirits high is to elicit the support of your intuitive guidance. Through this practice of self-awareness and self-exploration, you can ask your guardian angels and spirit guides for the support, clarity or guidance you will need along your journey.

The last step of the manifestation process is allowing aligned opportunities to present themselves in divine timing. Sometimes it can feel like you've been waiting forever for a certain goal to manifest. Maybe you start to doubt that your goals are even possible. It's really easy to give up or change direction when you don't have physical evidence that your efforts are effective. But don't fall into that trap.

It's the same trap that causes millions of people to die without fulfilling their purpose or goals in life. This step requires a great deal of patience, faith and focus. If you stay committed and focused on your goals, they will eventually manifest. According to the Law of Attraction, the universe will always match your energy. If you're filled with doubt, fear and indecision around your desires, this will show up in your energy and delay their fulfillment.

Know and trust with all your heart and soul that you deserve and are capable of creating the life you dream about. This level of confidence in your dreams will create a clear channel of communication between you and the universe. When you do this consistently, the universe will have no choice but to give you what you want. The following are a few useful manifesting techniques that you can practice.

VISUALISATION

Visualisation is one of the best techniques you can use. When you do a creative visualisation exercise, you imagine doing what you want to manifest, right? Well, you can also do visualisations from a third person perspective, seeing yourself from the outside. In fact, studies show that sports stars often improve their skills most effectively by seeing themselves in their visualisations.

Try alternating the perspective you use and see which gets the best results. For what it is worth, many people find the third person perspective the best, although it may take some getting used to if you've always conducted visualisations from the first person.

As well as changing up your perspective when you're visualising, it's so important that you learn how to do multi-sensory visualisations. What I mean is that you need to involve more than just your sense of sight when you're picturing your dream life. Use all of your senses to create a maximally vivid picture. What sounds can you hear? What does the environment smell like? If you touch objects or a person, what do they feel like under your hands? The more sensory experiences you invoke, the more potent your manifestation attempt will become. It's better to have a succinct, rich visualisation that's full of sensory data than it is to have a long-winded visualisation that chronicles days rather than just one amazing moment.

AFFIRMATIONS

Affirmations are another popular technique used by both beginners and experts. In the simple terms, the definition of affirmations, which are sometimes called 'self-affirmations', is using 'positive sentences that you repeat to yourself' to build up self-belief in the subconscious mind. This means effectively writing a list of affirmations that inspire and motivate you to be better and help to overcome inner barriers and self-doubt.

When you first start saying these phrases, they might not necessarily be true. But they should be designed to reflect what you want to be true, not what you are. You need to make them powerful and unique to who and what you want to become. Then over time, the consistent repetition of daily positive affirmations will help to reshape your inner beliefs and assumptions about yourself and the world around you. This reshaping gives you a more positive perception of who you are and where you stand. So most importantly, you have to truly believe an affirmation to be true.

INTENTION POINT

The 'Intention Point' is possibly the best-kept secret of the Law of Attraction. Most of my success has come directly from gaining a better understanding of what the intention point is and from learning how to adjust it in order to communicate a more coherent, strong message to the universe. In some senses, intention point techniques are the only ones you'll ever really need to properly use the Law of Attraction. Your intention point is basically the 'meeting ground' between your heart and your mind, your thoughts and your emotions. When you activate your intention point you manifest from a higher energy vibration, so things come faster and easier.

DREAM BOARDS

Dream boards are another great technique, which involve getting a board, or clearing a wall space and using it to display pictures and words that encapsulate what you want to manifest. So, for example, if you want to attract a new love into your life, you might cut out some magazine images of happy couples, locations you'd like to visit, food you'd eat together, and words that strike a chord with you. Be creative, because you can also include your own drawings, written phrases or even things you find in nature! Be sure to place your dream board in a prominent location where you'll see it multiple times a day.

Finally, if you're a beginner to manifestation you are encouraged to read 'The Secret' by Rhonda Byrne [1]. Additionally, it's important to start out small and build your confidence. Don't expect yourself to accumulate millions overnight. Have fun, and undertake small manifestations that you believe you can achieve in a reasonable time frame eg: finding a rose, being given a cup of coffee, etc.

Manifestation and how you can use it to ward off negative energy, is a valuable tool for creating a beautiful life for yourself. It helps us to understand that there's nothing that can stop you from living your desired, positive life.

CHAPTER SIXTEEN

◆

Synchronicities

The concept of 'synchronicities' was briefly touched upon in chapter ten. However, it's profound impact warrants dealing with the subject in much more depth. This chapter will cover what synchronicities are, what their purpose is, ways they show up in our lives and how to manifest more of them into life.

The term 'synchronicity' was originally coined by psychologist Carl Jung, and refers to the meaningful, or even miraculous coincidences that occur throughout your life. When you experience synchronicity, you'll have experiences that seem far too significant to be mere day-to-day serendipitous encounters. Synchronicity can manifest itself in an endless number of forms eg: popular names, numbers, words, symbols and events. Some could also call a synchronicity, a sign from God.

Roderick Main, in 'Jung on Synchronicity and the Paranormal' stated clearly that, "The culmination of Jung's lifelong engagement with the paranormal is his theory of synchronicity, the view that the structure of reality includes a principle of a causal connection which manifests itself most conspicuously in the form of meaningful coincidences. Difficult, flawed, prone to misrepresentation, this theory none-the-less remains one of the most suggestive attempts yet made to bring the paranormal within the bounds of intelligibility. It has been found relevant by psychotherapists, parapsychologists, researchers of spiritual experience and a growing number of non-specialists. Indeed, Jung's writings in this area form an excellent general introduction to the whole field of the paranormal."

An excellent example of synchronicity is where a person may dream of a symbol, such as a heart and then receive a card in the mail from their first love, the very next day with the same heart on it. The coincidence being the appearance of the heart in the dream and then again on the card. The meaning is derived from the feelings, thoughts and actions it inspires. The symbol may be a sign or reminder about the shared heart connection. If the person decides to call and reconnect with their first love, this is synchronicity! Synchronicity is when a coincidence shifts the motion of your life. Coincidence in action is synchronicity.

What is the purpose of synchronicity? A growing number of people believe that synchronicity is like a powerful 'wink' from the universe telling us that we're on the right track. Synchronicity is also believed to be a form of guidance from the 'higher self' and is a way of showing you where to go and what to do next in your life, as you proceed through your spiritual awakening.

The reason synchronicities are there is to make us feel something, and the feeling that our lives are rich and worth our reflection comes in part from our sense of the depth and mystery of life. In fact, maybe the most important thing synchronicities offer is astonishment. After all, how often in the course of a day, a week or a month, do you find yourself thunderstruck, flabbergasted at life, amazed by its finesse?

Synchronicities are like the glimpse of a wild animal seldom seen, the discovery of an ancient arrowhead or a geode, the return of your purse by some good Samaritan. Far removed from the mundane that seems to characterise such a vast portion of daily life, synchronicities help reconnect you to your sense of awe, and given the tyranny of the commonplace, what a service!

No one has been able to fully explain synchronicity, so perhaps you should simply accept it as a wild card and an ordering principle. It is the height of absurdity and the depth of profundity, and a crack in the door through which you can catch sight of the universe and its mysterious ways. You might be wondering how synchronicities show up. Well, they come in many different and unique ways, and they are often tailor-made for us. However, there are some common synchronicities that many people may experience.

Synchronicities are the moments when our 'higher self' attempts to establish a magical connection! It's the moment we actually get a taste of our divine nature. When this happens, our cells and our astral bodies are synchronised with the universe and therefore we channel very important messages for us and our lives, as well as the ones we love. They are messages we cannot receive in another way, and are windows of opportunity.

When synchronicities occur, we may get this very intense feeling that time bends, creating time to act and connect more. We should focus on their signals to magnify their effect, since they don't happen often if we neglect them. What are the different types of synchronicities?

Déjà Vu

Déjà vu is an important synchronicity that we often brush off. Déjà vu is a feeling that you have experienced an event or place before. It is unique and fundamentally different from everything else. Déjà vu occurs when you go about your day, minding your own business and seemingly nothing special is happening. You go somewhere new, and suddenly it hits you... that weird sensation of familiarity! You overwhelmingly feel you've been here or have experienced this before. Or have you?

Déjà vu is a subject that has been ignored for a long time and even considered too spooky or flaky to explore. But even though there is no official or scientific explanation of this phenomenon, it is very possible that it just means that this situation, event or place is significant enough to you, to have the universe make you stop and think about it. It draws your attention to a specific moment in time.

It is definitely a sign, as opposed to something that otherwise you wouldn't have noticed at all. The problems are that it is often a sign that is very hard to decipher. If you experience déjà vu, there are two things you should do.

First, you should meditate. In other words, free up some mental space in order to make the déjà vu stronger and clearer. Only this way will you be able to understand what exactly the universe is trying to tell you. This eerie feeling can go away extremely quickly, which is why your mind needs to be uncluttered by other things, in order for you to seize this moment and really find the message. Meditation will achieve this state.

You need to let your mind switch off and re-boot once in a while, and you should meditate on the experience. And don't worry as this need not be the boring traditional meditation. You don't have to sit in an uncomfortable lotus position. The number of times you will need to repeat this depends on when your next déjà vu happens and how much you will be able to get out of it. The meditation also helps you to release stress and anxiety, and boost energy levels. So, meditation is great for everyday life, not just when you are looking for a sign from the universe.

Second on your list is to keep a little déjà vu journal. Even though, like with dreams, you may forget it as soon as it happens, try to record as many details as you can like, what was it? Where were you when it happened? What time of day was it? What did you see? What were you doing? Who was you with? What were you thinking about?

After a while, you may realise that there is a similar topic to your various déjà vu records. Maybe you are always around the same person when it happens. In that case, it might mean that this person could be your soulmate. Or maybe, this person can point you in the right direction in your life.

Also, compare your déjà vu notes to your dream boards and visualisations. Is there any connection? And finally, take special note of how it made you feel. Déjà vu is a really weird sensation, and it can be very hard to explain how it made us feel. But try to notice your overall mood. Were you excited, scared, bored?

For example, if you are getting déjà vu at work and it is making you feel frustrated, it might be a sign that you are not where you are meant to be, maybe it is time to find a new job. On the other hand, if you feel excited, it may be a sign that you are on the right track.

ANIMALS

As discussed in chapter ten, another common synchronicity is animals, who are the agents of our Mother Earth. Every species vibrates on a its own special frequency. When the time is right, animals are attracted by cosmic signals, attracting them to special places in order to deliver a message. Some animals are harbingers of doom, or divine intervention. Other animals may perform certain mannerisms or moving patterns, which may form special kinds of symbols or runes. But if animals follow you, or seem to be attracted by your presence, you may want to contact the 'Totem Animal' of this species and ask why this is happening.

COINCIDENCE

Another amazing synchronicity is thinking of someone and then seeing them, or receiving an unexpected phone call. It may have been a while since you last talked to one of your old friends, but despite all the many different things happening in your life, you are somehow thinking of them. Then, amazingly... very soon afterwards, you actually greet them in the streets, or you receive a call or text from them! Is this just a coincidence? No of course not, it can't be.

Do you know what the chances are of this happening? Well, it's more possible to win the lottery. But why is this happening? Evidence suggests it may occur because you developed a strong telepathic link, which actually led to this amazing communication, attracting each other.

If this kind of coincidence begins happening, you should probably start trying to develop your telepathic abilities. Moreover, you should try to figure out, why did this happen with this particular person. What does this person symbolise for you? Could this be an omen of something? Hearing the answer to a question that bothers you from a stranger, or you are bothered by something, yet you don't know what is the right answer. And then suddenly, someone is saying something on the phone, which you accidentally overhear, or they come up and speak to you. Could what they just said be the answer to your question?

It's very common to accidentally receive a solution from a random stranger who is speaking to his friend or saying something on the phone. They often say that God works in mysterious ways, so this might be a divine intervention, or it could be the 'voice of God' speaking directly to you. If this happens, try to remember the conversation. Observe what is happening around this stranger, what they're wearing, and memorise the message and the colours which may actually serve as messengers.

DREAMS

Synchronicities occur when you see or hear about something that happened in your dreams. The interesting thing is that some dreams produce far more synchronicities than you might normally notice. The theme of a dream is its 'motif'. However, if you look deeper, you'll often see your motif dream symbol repeating the next day in a modified or cryptic form. When you experience synchronicity, go back to the dream and interpret it thoroughly, because the theme of the dream is so powerful that it has already symbolically manifested in your life.

Many people think of synchronicity as a positive sign to follow, but this is not necessarily so. It is a symbol shouting loudly from your dream, spilling into your waking life. It is the symbolic beginning of a manifestation. If you interpret your dream and you like the way the wind is blowing, follow the signs. If you don't like the way the wind is blowing, apply some dream alchemy and change your future.

NUMEROLOGY

By far and away the most common signs of synchronicity are numbers, and they often hold the most meaning. Numerology is a study of its own, and this section covers what numbers have to do with synchronicities. Numbers are ancient, meaningful and powerful. It was the Pythagoreans in the 6th century BC who were one of the first groups to popularise the idea that numbers are not merely mathematical symbols, but they actually carry spiritual significance. As Pythagoras was once quoted as saying, "number is the ruler of forms and ideas and the cause of gods and daemons".

Thanks to Pythagoras, we have a system of numerology which ascribes different meanings to numbers. But numerology is only one side of the coin, because numbers have been given special meanings all throughout history, religion and cultural mythology. From the Far East to our own Western heritage, numbers have carried meaning for millennia.

How many times have you seen repetitive numbers such as 11:11, 777, 1010, 4444, 999 and so forth? Seeing repetitive numbers is a form of synchronicity. These numbers are sometimes called angel numbers. As an example, this year is 2020 and today happens to be June 1st, but what's more is that I have been seeing 11 and 11:11 several times a day for about six months now. Although I am having trouble doing as I'm told, I know what my angel is trying to tell me, and I will get there, but I know they will keep sending me these numbers until I obey.

All throughout history, numbers have come to mean many different things to different cultures. However, overall, numbers have been given similar meanings. Take the number four, for example. The native Americans believe that there are four winds and four directions. Along a similar line, the Ancient Greeks believed that there were four elements. In Christianity, four is the number of creation i.e. on the fourth day of the week God finished creating the material universe. This simple example reveals that the number four has a very similar meaning across three completely different time periods and cultures. Even in Tarot cards, the numbers have significance.

It's important to note however, that while it's beneficial to find out the general meaning of numbers, it is imperative that you find out your personal meaning behind it. Synchronicity, symbolism and the meaning of numbers are all extremely personal, so be wary of prescribing a meaning to your life that is not actually correct or relevant. It can be tempting to not put in any work and just go with what the traditional meaning of the number is, but don't do this. It's much better through a little effort, to explore what the meaning of numbers are for you. The following actions are a few ways to find out what each number could mean for you and its context.

Write down every word association you can think of for each number. For instance, if you keep seeing the number 2 you might write, 'male and female, relationships, yin and yang, duality, light and dark, up and down, material and spiritual' and so on.

After seeing a series of repetitive numbers, you might immediately have a thought or inkling about what the number means. Don't ignore this immediate interpretation, but write down what pops into your mind. Often the meanings we first ascribe to these numbers and patterns are the truest because little mental effort is involved. The more mental effort, the more we start fabricating meanings.

What interpretation triggers strong feelings within you? My answer is to pay attention to how triggering that interpretation is. For example, does your analysis stir up feelings of excitement, awe, fear, jubilation or even just send tingles down your spine? This is a good sign that you've found the right explanation, because your body is reacting in such a heightened way. However, if the interpretation you have feels cold, flat or detached… it's probably the wrong fit.

The following is a general consensus that mythology, religion, mysticism and esotericism have formulated about each number. It is important to emphasise that you find your own meanings, but it does help at the outset to know what each number means. Sometimes we tune into the traditional energy, magic and meaning of each number, but note that the repetition of numbers emphasises their meaning. For example, 1111 is more powerful than seeing 11.

Zero is representative of the primordial void, the womb, the realm of potential. Zero is a circle that symbolises totality, that which precedes life, the eternal force. It is nothing and everything, the beginning and the end. Zero is often symbolic of spirit or God, and hence of unity and wholeness.

One symbolises leadership, strength and confidence. Number one is like a straight arrow which reflects willpower and precision. One is also reflective of individuality, self-discovery and self-empowerment. Unlike zero, which is feminine and receptive, one has a masculine and a wilful energy.

Two is the number of dualities, the split we perceive in life between light and darkness, inside and outside, yin and yang, masculine and feminine, good and bad, life and death, mind and heart and so on. On one hand, two symbolises partnership, but on the other it symbolises conflict and opposition. When balanced, two is a number of harmonies, but when imbalanced the number two can be destructive.

Three is typically seen as a particularly lucky and powerful number. Three represents the divine principle that underlies life such as the mind, body and spirit; birth, life and death; beginning, middle and end; past, present and future, and so forth. Spiritual traditions such as Wicca and Christianity symbolise the spiritual force as a triune, for example, the Father, Son and Holy

Spirit, as well as the Maiden, Mother and Crone. Three is symbolic of success, intuition and good fortune.

Four is a grounded and stable number that evokes a feeling of calmness and solidity. Four is very much rooted in the physical world and is about being present and in the 'now.' For example, there are four seasons, four elements, and four corners of the earth. Four is about building a strong foundation and developing a down-to-earth perspective.

Five is a number of adventure and freedom. Five is also a very sensual number (five senses, five fingers and toes) and it's about enjoying life, trying new experiences and seeking out pleasure. This number is also connected to experiencing life changes such as marriage, divorce, new jobs and making important choices.

Six represents a balance between the earthly and spiritual realms. Six is also connected to intuition, clairvoyance and other extrasensory capacities, hence the 'sixth' sense. In numerology, six is the number of the caretaker; the person who nurtures and compassionately serves others.

Seven is a magical number that is associated with synchronicity, luck and perfection eg: seven chakras, seven colours of the rainbow, seven days in the week. Seven is also seen as a mystical number that is connected to spiritual awakening, introspection and the development of wisdom. This number is connected with the pursuit of truth and the desire for a deeper understanding of life.

Eight is connected to abundance, prosperity and financial well-being. Resourcefulness, hard work, determination and inner strength are all qualities of eight. Spiritually, eight is seen as an equaliser or balancer, hence its shape that unites the conscious with the unconscious, and earthly with the spiritual. In other words, eight is reflected in the proverb, 'you will reap what you sow'.

Nine is the number of fulfillments. Wisdom, self-examination, enlightenment, and higher consciousness are all qualities associated with number nine. Nine is also connected to one's higher purpose and ultimate life mission, which encourages us to take a bird's eye view of our lives.

Ten represents completion, the ending of a cycle and the attainment of wholeness. Ten is both masculine and feminine and reflects the unity that is possible once we integrate the fragmented pieces of our inner selves.

Eleven is a powerful number that is often referred to as the 'spiritual messenger.' This number carries with it both positive and negative associations. On one hand, eleven can represent the need to make an urgent change, hence the saying 'the eleventh hour', but on the other, eleven is connected with one's destiny. In other words, seeing eleven can tell you a lot about your life path and what paths you should or shouldn't walk.

Twelve is the number of cosmic orders. For example, there are twelve months in the year, twelve astrological signs, twelve hours in a day, twelve personality archetypes. According to numerology, twelve is the number of creative and individualistic self-expression.

Understanding the meaning of numbers gives you that extra layer of insight when it comes to self-discovery and realisation. While the personal meaning you assign to numbers might not always conform to the above descriptions, I hope these explanations help to shed some insight.

THE ANGEL NUMBER

Digressing briefly, the number 1111 warrants a more in-depth analysis, since this is a very powerful number to see in your waking life. Angel numbers 1111 are about new beginnings and starting over. If you feel like your life is going nowhere, think of these angel numbers as a wake-up call. If you keep seeing the numbers 1111 repeatedly, expect little miracles and happy coincidences to happen more frequently in your life. Most of the time, these numbers appear when you are about to experience a spiritual awakening or rebirth of some sort.

These numbers usually make themselves known in your physical world in the most mundane things. You can see them everywhere you go, and it may feel like a coincidence most of the time. They can appear on a random license plate, a digital clock, in the book you're reading, or on a show you're watching. They can appear anytime and anywhere, but they're never a coincidence. This is your angel's way of communicating with you that a bigger change is about to happen.

Seeing the number 1111 signifies that energy doorways have been opened. You will soon experience a shift in your life energy when you turn your thoughts into reality. Your angels want you to know that you should choose the kind of thoughts you put in your head, that reflect what you truly desire. Don't focus on the things that scare you or keep you from reaching your full potential. You can end up making those fears a reality. The next time you see the angel number 1111, make a wish! Send your deepest desires to the universe and watch how your angel numbers will work for you.

The meaning of number 1111 encourages you to create new beginnings, make new opportunities, and work on new projects with a strong and positive attitude. It wants you to know that you should start turning your dreams into reality. It's a confirmation that your desires are about to get real. Keep your thoughts positive and you will attract only big and positive things. Pay attention to what's happening around you because your angels are trying to reach out to you.

The meaning of number 1111 is also synchronicity. More than just happy coincidences, angel numbers really tell you the answers that you need to hear. Angel numbers 1111 symbolise that the universe has opened an energy doorway for you. The universe has recognised you and is reaching out to help.

However, these are just a few amongst many examples. There are many other combinations of numbers that hold meaning, eg: 2323, which is a mix of the numbers 2 and 3. If it's in a pattern, it has a meaning.

A knowledge of the many different synchronicities is important, but how can you bring more of them into your life?

1. Increase Your Awareness

When you truly open your eyes to what's happening around you through people, nature, sounds and smell, suddenly the world comes alive and takes a different form. One of the easiest ways to do this is to simply practice conscious breathing and allow yourself to enjoy whatever you're doing, even if it's not completely pleasant, like when sitting in traffic. Take advantage of these solitary moments to connect with something greater than yourself and soon you'll start opening your heart to receiving more signs from the universe.

2. Ask Questions

Synchronicity is a powerful source of guidance, so why not use it for your own good? If you're looking for answers, or if you can't figure out what your passion or purpose is in life, simply place your intention in the universe and then wait for the answers. It may come in the form of numbers, a message or some specific advice, but make sure you've opened up your awareness so you can find the answers you're seeking.

3. Surrender

Release your need to anticipate your desired future and just surrender to the outcome. Remember that you attract whatever you focus your intention on, so if there's a challenge that you're going through right now, release the worry and let synchronicity take over.

4. Practice Gratitude

Deepak Chopra once said, "Gratitude opens the door to the power, the wisdom, the creativity of the universe. You open the door through gratitude", and I couldn't agree more. When we stop appreciating the beauty that surrounds us, we lose sight of what's truly important. Every time you practice gratitude, you'll not only be acknowledging the power outside of you, but you'll also unleash your own potential. When this happens, you achieve flow and therefore, synchronicity follows you.

5. Trust

When you start trusting your intuition, you start developing a better relationship with yourself and your inner guidance system. When this happens, you'll experience a much deeper alignment with the universe and opportunities will unfold. You'll meet the right people and you'll feel you're always at the right place at the right time. The truth is, life is full of opportunities, you just need to be willing to see them!

Synchronicities are a beautiful part of life that lead us to where we are truly meant to be. They're all around us, and they're just a small nudge from God, the angels and our spirit guides, to help us along the way.

CHAPTER SEVENTEEN

◆

Meditation

Meditation is a practice that will help heal you in multiple ways. It has beautiful physical, mental and emotional benefits, and is an important aspect of connecting to God, warding off evil spirits and living a beautiful life.

Meditation is a mental exercise that involves relaxation, focus and awareness. The practice is usually done individually, in a still, seated position with eyes closed. Meditation is to the mind what physical exercise is to the body. In psychology, meditation is defined as, 'a family of mental training practices that are designed to familiarise the practitioner with specific types of mental processes'.

Meditation is practiced in one of three general modes. Concentration, which focuses attention on a single object, internal or external, otherwise known as 'focused attention meditation'. Observation, or paying attention to whatever is predominant in your experience at that present moment, without allowing the attention to get stuck on any particular thing, and is known as 'open monitoring meditation'. And awareness, which allows consciousness to remain present, undistracted and not engaged with either focusing or observing.

Other characteristics of meditation are that it is an individual practice, even if done in groups, such as in a meditation retreat. Meditation is often performed with eyes closed, but not always, as both Zazen and Trataka are examples of open-eye styles of meditation. Meditation usually involves bodily stillness. But there are also ways to do walking meditation, and to integrate 'mindfulness' in other activities.

Originally, the word 'meditate' actually meant to think deeply about something. However, when Eastern contemplative practices were exported to Western cultures, this is the term that was used to define them, for lack of a better word. Nowadays, meditation has more the meaning of this exercise of focusing attention than to reflect deeply.

Definitions of meditation can also be found in religion. In Christianity, meditation is a type of contemplative prayer that creates a sense of union with God, or the contemplation of religious themes. Whereas in Buddhism, meditation is one of the three core practices for the purification of mind and attainment of Nirvana.

There are many things in life that are beyond our control. However, it is possible to take responsibility for our own states of mind, and to change them for the better. According to Buddhism this is the most important thing we can do. Buddhism teaches that it is the only real antidote to our own personal sorrows, and to the anxieties, fears, hatreds, and general confusions that beset the human condition.

As a means of transforming the mind, Buddhist meditation practices are techniques that encourage and develop concentration, clarity, emotional positivity, and a calm seeing of the true nature of things. By engaging with a particular meditation practice, you learn the patterns and habits of your mind, and the practice offers a means to cultivate new, more positive ways of being. With regular work and patience, a focused condition can deepen into a profoundly peaceful and energised state of mind. Such experiences can have a transformative effect and lead to a new understanding of life. Over the millennia, countless meditation practices have been developed in the Buddhist tradition.

Besides focus of attention, meditation also involves mental calmness and introspection, or 'looking within'. Meditation is thus somewhat different than other personal development or spiritual exercises, like:

- Affirmation, self-hypnosis, or guided visualisation, where the objective is more to imprint a specific message on the mind
- Pure relaxation, where the goal is only to release bodily tensions
- Prayer, where there is a conscious flow of thinking and feeling, directed towards a deity
- Contemplation, where the thought processes is actively engaged in order to deepen the understanding of a subject or concept
- Trance dancing — where the main goal is usually to produce visions or an altered state of consciousness
- Breathing exercises like 'pranayama' and most types of 'qigong', where the focus is on producing

a certain pattern of breathing and purify the body

All these practices are also therapeutic and helpful, but they are different from meditation, although some meditation techniques may make use of some of these elements.

The Benefits of Meditation

Meditation is beneficial in several ways, and it has different uses for different people. However, what drives people to practice meditation falls into three main categories:

- Specific benefits: improving your health, wellbeing, performance or focus
- Growth: emotional healing, self-knowledge, self-discipline and letting go
- Spirituality: connecting with God, inner peace and other spiritual goals

Whatever drives you to meditate, the benefits you seek will accrue from the proportion of consistency and commitment to building the habit. But 'the wider you cast your net, the more fish you will get', so I would encourage you to practice not only for one particular reason, but for the sake of the practice itself. The following is a list of benefits that meditation can deliver.

1. Reduces Stress

Stress reduction is one of the most common reasons people turn to meditation. One study including over

3,500 adults showed that it lives up to its reputation for stress reduction. Normally, mental and physical stress cause increased levels of the stress hormone cortisol. This produces many of the harmful effects of stress, such as the release of inflammation-promoting chemicals called cytokines. The effect of cytokines can disrupt sleep, promote depression and anxiety, increase blood pressure and contribute to fatigue and cloudy thinking.

In an eight-week study, a meditation style called 'mindfulness meditation' reduced the inflammation response caused by stress. Another study in nearly 1,300 adults demonstrated that meditation may decrease stress. Notably, this effect was strongest in individuals with the highest levels of stress. Research has shown that meditation may also improve symptoms of stress-related conditions, including irritable bowel syndrome, post-traumatic stress disorder and fibromyalgia.

2. Controls Anxiety

Less stress translates to less anxiety. For example, an eight-week study of mindfulness meditation helped participants reduce their anxiety. It also reduced symptoms of anxiety disorders, such as phobias, social anxiety, paranoid thoughts, obsessive-compulsive behaviours and panic attacks. Another study followed up with 18 volunteers three years after they had completed an eight-week meditation program. Most volunteers had continued practicing regular meditation and maintained lower anxiety levels over the long term.

An even larger study of 2,466 participants showed that a variety of different meditation strategies may reduce anxiety levels. For example, yoga has been shown to help people reduce anxiety. This is likely due to benefits from both meditative practice and physical activity. Meditation may also help control job-related anxiety in high-pressure work environments, and one study found that a meditation program reduced anxiety in a group of nurses.

3. Promotes Emotional Health

Some forms of meditation can also lead to an improved self-image and more positive outlook on life. Inflamed cytokines, which are released in response to stress, can also affect mood, leading to depression. A review of several studies suggests meditation may reduce depression by decreasing these inflammatory chemicals.

Two studies of mindfulness meditation found decreased depression in over 4,600 adults. Another study followed 18 volunteers as they practiced meditation over three years also found that participants experienced long-term decreases in depression. Another controlled study compared electrical activity between the brains of people who practiced mindfulness meditation and the brains of others who did not. Those who meditated showed measurable changes in activity in areas related to positive thinking and optimism.

4. Enhances Self-awareness

Some forms of meditation may help you develop a stronger understanding of yourself, helping you grow into your best self. For example, 'self-inquiry meditation' explicitly aims to help you develop a greater understanding of yourself and how you relate to those around you. Other forms teach you to recognise thoughts that may be harmful or self-defeating. The idea is that as you gain greater awareness of your thought habits, you can steer them toward more constructive patterns.

A study of 21 women fighting breast cancer found that when they took part in a Tai Chi program, their self-esteem improved more than it did than in those who received social support sessions. In another study, 40 senior men and women who took a mindfulness meditation program experienced reduced feelings of loneliness, compared to a control group that had been placed on a wait list for the program. Also, experience in meditation may cultivate more creative problem solving.

5. Can Generate Kindness

Some types of meditation may particularly increase positive feelings and actions toward yourself and others. Metta, a type of meditation also known as Loving-kindness meditation, begins with developing kind thoughts and feelings toward yourself. Through practice, people learn to extend this kindness and forgiveness externally, first to friends, then to acquaintances and ultimately enemies.

Twenty-two studies of this form of meditation have demonstrated its ability to increase peoples' compassion toward themselves and others. One study of 100 adults randomly assigned to a program that included loving-kindness meditation found that these benefits were dose-dependent. In other words, the more effort people put into Metta meditation, the more positive feelings they experienced. Another group of studies showed the positive feelings people develop through Metta meditation can improve social anxiety, reduce marriage conflict and help anger management. These benefits also appear to accumulate over time with the practice of loving-kindness meditation.

Whatever the reason for taking up meditation, your motivation to do so may also evolve over time, as the practice starts to unfold in your life.

Meditation Misconceptions
Although the media has made meditation quite popular, there are a number of misconceptions surrounding its practice, with much 'fake news' and fabricated information coming out of it.

1. You don't need to have a mantra, but you can have one if you want.

It has become common for people to confuse mantra with the idea of an intention or specific words to live by. A motto. But the actual word 'mantra' means something quite different, because a mantra is a 'mind-vehicle'. Mantras can be used in meditation as a tool to help your mind enter, or remain in your meditation practice. Other types of meditation use techniques like sound, counting breaths or even just the breath itself as a concentrating tool. Another way to think about a mantra is like an anchor, since it holds your mind as you meditate and can be what you come back to when your thoughts invariably wander.

2. Don't expect your brain to go blank.

One of the biggest misconceptions about meditation is that your mind is supposed to go blank and that you reach a super-Zen state of consciousness. This is typically not true, and it's important to keep in mind that you don't have to try to clear thoughts from your brain during meditation.

According to Deepak Chopra, a meditation expert and founder of the Chopra Center for Wellbeing, "The nature of the mind to move from one thought to another is in fact the very basis of meditation. We don't eliminate the tendency of the mind to jump from one thought to another. That's not possible anyway".

Depending on the type of meditation you learn, there are techniques for gently bringing your focus back to your meditation practice. Alternatively, some types of meditation actually emphasise being present and mindful to thoughts as they arise as part of the practice.

3. You don't have to sit with your legs crossed.

You can sit in any position that is comfortable, and most people sit upright in a chair or on a cushion. Your hands can fall gently in your lap or at your sides. It is best not to lie down unless you're doing a body scan meditation or meditation for sleep.

4. It's okay if you fall asleep.

It's very common to doze off during meditation and some believe that the brief sleep you get is actually very restorative. It's not the goal, but if it's a by-product of your meditation, that is okay. Other practices might give tricks on how to stay more alert if you fall asleep, like sitting upright in a chair. In our experience, the relaxation that can come from meditation is a wonderful thing, and if that means a mini-snooze, so be it.

5. There are many ways to learn.

With meditation becoming so available to the masses, people can learn how to meditate alone, in a group, on a retreat, with their phone or even by listening to guided meditations online. Everyone has a different learning style and there are plenty of options out there to fit individual needs.

6. You can meditate for general wellness.

Some meditation exercises are aimed at one goal, like helping to ease anxiety or helping people who have trouble sleeping. One popular mindfulness meditation technique known as the 'Loving-kindness meditation', previously mentioned in point 5, promotes the positive act of wishing ourselves or others happiness. However, if you don't have a specific goal in mind, you can still reap the benefits of the practice.

7. Meditation has so many health benefits.

Meditation can help boost the immune system, reduce stress and anxiety, improve concentration, decrease blood pressure, improve your sleep, increase your happiness, and has even helped people deal with alcohol or smoking addictions.

8. Meditation can physically change your brain.

Researchers have not only looked at the brains of meditators and non-meditators to study the differences, but they have also started looking at a group of brains before and after eight weeks of mindfulness meditation. Forbes magazine reported that the results were remarkable because the scientists noted everything from, "changes in grey matter volume to reduced activity in the 'me' centres of the brain, to enhanced connectivity between brain regions".

Those who participated in an eight-week mindfulness program also showed signs of a shrinking of the amygdala, the brain's 'fight or flight' center, as well as a thickening of the pre-frontal cortex, which handles brain functions like concentration and awareness.

Researchers also looked at the brain imaging of long-term, experienced meditators. Many, when not in a state of meditation, had brain image results that looked more like the images of a regular person's brain while meditating. In other words, the experienced meditator's cortex is remarkably different than the non-meditator's brain.

9. Mindfulness and meditation are not the same thing.

These two concepts are talked about in conjunction often because one form of meditation is called mindfulness meditation. But mindfulness is defined most loosely as cultivating a present awareness in your everyday life. One way to do this is through meditation, however not all meditation practices necessarily focus on mindfulness. Mindfulness meditation is referred to most often when experts talk about the health benefits of meditation.

10. You have enough time to meditate.

While some formal meditation practices call for 20 minutes, twice a day, many other meditation exercises can be as short as five or ten minutes. We easily spend that amount of time flipping through Netflix or liking things on Instagram. For some, it's as simple as setting the morning alarm ten minutes earlier, or getting off your computer a few minutes before dinner to practice.

Another way to think about incorporating meditation into your daily routine is likening it to brushing your teeth. You might not do it at the exact same time each morning, but you always make sure you brush your teeth before you leave the house for the day. For those who start to see the benefits of daily meditation, it becomes a non-negotiable part of their routine.

Armed with good understanding of what meditation is, and the benefits it can produce, are there different methods of conducting meditation? Because this book is about the supernatural, a protective meditation is an important one to know.

1. Protective Meditation

If you're facing a negative energy or spirit in your house, or you are simply in a negative mood, this meditation can help, because it is a strong clearing meditation.

Before clearing any space, you should clear your own energy. Just as you regularly cleanse your body, it's important to cleanse the funky, gunky energy that's in your field. Some of it will invariably be yours from your own stress, illness, or painful emotions, and some will be what you've picked up from other people and entities.

Think of it as energy hygiene. As much as you don't want the spirit in your house, you don't want it attached to you either. If you are religious or spiritual, you can ask for divine help for this process too.

Set an intention for releasing all your own negative energy and everything you've picked up from others. I like to say, "I am easily releasing all energy from myself and others that no longer serves me. I do this for my highest good".

Then... imagine a small ball of brilliant, golden light in the centre of your chest, expanding the light on each exhalation. Imagine breathing in and out through your chest, expanding the light on each exhalation. Spread the light throughout your entire body. Visualise it in your head, torso, arms and toes. Now expand it beyond your skin until the light is about an arm's length out in all directions.

Follow by shielding. Imagine a large bubble around you, about an arm's length from your body in all directions. See this bubble as a solid wall or a filter that covers you completely. Ask this bubble, or shield to act as a cell wall, using its intelligence to allow love and positive energy in. Ask that anything negative not be allowed in, to hit the shield, slide off and be neutralised by the Earth. (Another option is to imagine mirrors on the outside of the shield, so anything sent your way gets reflected back to the person who sent it. Frankly, I'd like less negative energy in the world and prefer my method above.)

Fill the bubble with golden light. This meditation is a great way to release your body of any negative energies within you, and also works as a protection against further negative energy.

2. Basic Beginner Meditation

A simple beginner meditation for use with health, spirituality and much more is a great way to start your meditation journey. Begin to meditate by learning one simple technique and practicing it every day. There is no right or wrong way to do it, since whatever resonates for you is the method you'll want to repeat. For one, you can try learning to meditate with this basic how-to technique, adapted from, 'Meditation for Dummies' by Stephan Bodian.

Sit comfortably on a cushion or a chair. Don't slouch, but your back doesn't need to be ramrod-straight either. At first, you may want to try sitting against a wall to support your back. Use extra pillows under your knees or anywhere else to make you comfortable. If sitting to meditate is unappealing then try lying down. Miriam Austin, author of 'Meditation for Wimps', recommends lying on the floor with your calves and feet resting on a chair seat.

You can put on music, if that helps to calm you before beginning to meditate, but turn it off once you begin. Set a digital (non-ticking) timer. Start with five minutes and work your way up to 10, then 15 and eventually 20 minutes. It will probably take weeks or months to lengthen the time you practice. Try not to put yourself on a schedule. Whatever pace you choose is fine. Breathe normally through your nose, with your mouth closed. Your eyes can be open or closed. Focus on the breath moving in and out of your nostrils, or on the rise and fall of your belly.

When you notice your mind wandering, bring it gently back to the breath. Be careful not to drift off because this is a temptation, especially if you're lying down. While shutting off your mind is not the goal of meditation, neither is judging the meditative process. No matter what feelings or thoughts you have, simply bring your focus back to the breath again... and again, as necessary.

3. Healing Meditation

Now that you have a basic beginner meditation, you can practice until you're a guru. Meditation may be difficult at first, because it's difficult to start teaching yourself to quiet your mind, when otherwise we think every second of every day. However, once you get the hang of it, it's quite pleasant and easy. Meditation is known to be one of the best health practices you can perform. It's almost like sleeping, as you rejuvenate your mind, body and soul. However, unlike sleeping, you can do it for just five minutes and it will still have a big impact on your life.

CHAPTER EIGHTEEN

◆

Post Traumatic Stress Disorder

Years of personal experience in dealing with torment dished out by demons, has left my heart and soul scarred and in physical terms my brain's mind. After going through those experiences, I still live in fear to this day. It was the hardest thing I've ever had to endure. Even writing this book was hard for me. It seemed that every time the wounds would heal, they'd somehow be reopened again. I'm not sure if that's because the demons were hiding, waiting for the moment that their presence would have a profound effect on me, or if they came into my life whenever I moved on and was less cautious.

How this affected me, however, was that I developed 'post-traumatic stress disorder' (PTSD). PTSD is a psychiatric disorder that occurs in people who have experienced or witnessed a traumatic event such as a natural disaster, a serious accident, a terrorist act, war/combat, rape or some other violent personal assault on themselves or someone else.

PTSD has been known by many names in the past, such as 'shell shock' during the years of World War I and 'combat fatigue' during World War II. But the affliction doesn't just happen to combat veterans. PTSD can occur in all people of any ethnicity, nationality, culture and at any age. PTSD affects approximately 3.5 percent of adults in the USA, and an estimated one in 11 people will be diagnosed with PTSD in their lifetime. Regrettably, women are twice as likely as men to develop PTSD.

People with PTSD develop intense, disturbing thoughts and feelings related to their experience that last long after the traumatic event has ended. They may relive the event through flashbacks or nightmares or feel sadness, fear or anger. They may also feel detached or estranged from other people. People with PTSD may avoid situations or people that remind them of the traumatic event, and they may have strong negative reactions to something as ordinary as a loud noise or an accidental touch that might trigger the memories.

A diagnosis of PTSD requires exposure to an upsetting traumatic event. However, exposure could be indirect rather than firsthand. For example, PTSD could occur in an individual learning about the violent death of a close family member. It can also occur as a result of repeated exposure to horrible details of trauma such as police officers exposed to details of child abuse cases.

The symptoms of PTSD are intrusive thoughts such as repeated, involuntary memories, distressing dreams, or flashbacks of the traumatic event. These flashbacks may be so vivid that people feel they are re-living the traumatic experience or seeing it before their eyes, all over again. Avoiding reminders of the traumatic event may include avoiding people, places, activities, objects and situations that bring on distressing memories. Sufferers may try to avoid remembering or thinking about the traumatic event. They may resist talking about what happened or how they feel about it.

Negative thoughts and feelings may include ongoing and distorted beliefs about oneself or others eg: "I am bad," and "no one can be trusted". Ongoing fear, horror, anger, guilt or shame, and a much-reduced interest in activities previously enjoyed, or feeling detached or estranged from others, are common effects. Arousal and reactive symptoms may include being irritable and having angry outbursts, behaving recklessly or in a self-destructive way, being easily startled, or having problems concentrating or sleeping.

Many people who have been exposed to a traumatic event, experience symptoms like those described above in the days following the event. However, a PTSD diagnosis requires symptoms that last for more than a month and persist for months and sometimes years. Many individuals develop symptoms within three months of the trauma, but symptoms may also appear later. For people with PTSD, the symptoms cause significant distress or functioning problems. PTSD often occurs in conjunction with other related conditions, such as depression, substance use, memory problems and other physical and mental health problems.

As this book is all about helping those who have been in the same or similar situations as I have, and have been afflicted by PTSD, it is both informative and useful to explore this condition and its treatments currently in use.

It is important to note that not everyone who experiences trauma develops PTSD, and not everyone who develops it requires psychiatric treatment. For some people, such as myself, symptoms of PTSD subside or disappear over time, although the fear may remain. Others recover with the help of family, friends or clergy. But many people with PTSD need professional care and treatment to recover from often intense and disabling psychological distress. It is important to remember that trauma may lead to severe distress. That distress is not the individual's fault, and PTSD is treatable. The earlier a person gets treatment, the greater the likeliness of a positive outcome.

Psychiatrists and other mental health professionals use various effective, and research-proven methods to help people recover from PTSD. Both psychotherapy and medication provide effective evidence-based treatments for PTSD. One category of psychotherapy, cognitive behaviour therapies (CBT), is very effective. Cognitive processing therapy, prolonged exposure therapy and stress inoculation therapy (described below) are among other types of CBT used to treat PTSD.

1. Cognitive Processing Therapy focuses on modifying painful negative emotions such as shame, guilt, etc., and beliefs, such as "I have failed," or "the world is dangerous", due to the trauma. Therapists help the person confront such distressing memories and emotions.

2. Prolonged Exposure Therapy uses repeated, detailed imagining of the trauma or progressive exposures to symptom 'triggers' in a safe, controlled way to help a person face and gain control of fear and distress and learn to cope.

For example, virtual reality programs have been used to help war veterans with PTSD re-experience the battlefield in a controlled, therapeutic way.

3. Group therapy encourages survivors of similar traumatic events to share their experiences and reactions in a comfortable and non-judgmental setting. Group members help one another realise that many people would have responded the same way and felt the same emotions. Family therapy may also help because the behaviour and distress of the person with PTSD can affect the entire family.

4. Other psychotherapies such as interpersonal, supportive and psychodynamic therapies focus on the emotional and interpersonal aspects of PTSD. These may be helpful for people who don't want to expose themselves to reminders of their traumas.

Acute stress disorder is related to PTSD but isn't PTSD. This disorder occurs in reaction to a traumatic event, just as PTSD does, and the symptoms are similar. However, the symptoms occur between three days and one month after the event. People with acute stress disorder may relive the trauma, have flashbacks or nightmares and may feel numb or detached from themselves. These symptoms cause major distress and cause problems in their daily lives. About half of people with acute stress disorder go on to have PTSD.

Psychotherapy, including cognitive behaviour therapy, can help control symptoms and help prevent them from getting worse and developing into PTSD.

When we hear the term PTSD, we automatically think about veterans who fought at war. However, PTSD can occur in just about anyone, for just about anything that goes wrong in life. Because my book is about the supernatural, I want to take a look at PTSD from paranormal experiences and how they have played out in my life and could play out in anyone else's life.

While researching, I found that PTSD can trigger paranormal activity, which is quite alarming for those who have developed PTSD from paranormal activity. Is it just an ongoing cycle? Maybe. However, when you think of it in more depth, it makes sense.

PTSD causes some unforgiving emotional issues, such as anger, sadness, or being scared. And as we discussed before, these negative feelings can attract demons and negative spirits. They essentially go hand-in-hand. PTSD is a difficult disorder to deal with, no matter the cause, because you feel scared every day. You're always on edge, waiting for the next horrific moment. That takes a toll on your body, mind and soul. However, because of the added paranormal activity, PTSD becomes even more difficult.

We've all heard of the rape victim who not only suffered a traumatic assault but who was further humiliated and/or disbelieved entirely. The fact is that most rapes go unreported and not just due to fear of being stigmatised, but also because it can be a natural reaction to trauma to simply shut down. One way of reacting to extreme stress, is in fact to dissociate completely and leave the body, sometimes viewing oneself from without.

This is a well-known phenomenon, especially in cases of childhood sexual abuse.

If this kind of natural response, confusion and fear of further humiliation can affect someone who has been traumatised in the 'real world', what then of the person who has had a terrifying paranormal experience? What happens to the hunter chased off his lease by a massive, eight-foot-tall Sasquatch? What happens to the alien abductee taken against her will and terrorised? What about the family subjected to poltergeist activity night after night? How about the child tormented by very real traumatic dreams of a violent death in a previous existence?

What happens to a person who feels forced to keep what may feel like the most momentous thing that's ever happened to them, a secret? The thing that they most feel the need for, which is compassion and support, is the very thing they don't receive for the very real fear of suffering further pain? What happens when that person is a child who wakes up to a strange figure at the foot of their bed but is told, "it's just a dream... get back in bed"?

> "It's often said that a traumatic experience early in life marks a person forever, pulls her out of line, saying, "Stay there. Don't move."
>
> – *Jeffrey Eugenides*

My guess is that the overwhelming majority of sufferers just keep quiet. Although my paranormal experiences have been life threatening and traumatising, it took years before I could ever speak about it. No one wants to be seen as a crazy person, however, I've decided to open up and talk about these life-long experiences to help those who have experienced the same kind of traumatic events.

It is my sincere hope that these affected people become more and more open and become more able to talk about their experiences openly and without fear of ridicule or rejection.

Maybe you're not sure if you're experiencing PTSD and whether or not to get help, but perhaps you can find a correlation between your own experience and what I went through. These days there are still a number of 'triggers' that spark off my PTSD anxieties.

The smell is that terrible and overwhelming sulphur odour that wafted in every time the demon was present. As soon as I detected it, my body would freeze. I'd become paralysingly afraid and couldn't move, breathe or think. All I could think was, "The demon is here". As a result of this, what do you think happens when I smell any awful smell now? Whether it just be the rubbish bin or any other bad smell that has a logical explanation. Of course, it scares me! My whole body goes into a panic and I freeze in absolute terror. I think to myself, "Not again", and become overwhelmingly sad, anxious and angry.

Abnormal noises are difficult to deal with, especially when it's dark and quiet. We've all heard noises in the night, whether it's just the old house moving and creaking, or a pet knocking something over. When that happens, you first listen quietly for what it may be. If the noise isn't repeated, most will brush it off and go back to sleep. But my response is very different, since I don't dare close my eyes for a second and will often stay awake all night. Imagine not sleeping every time you hear a noise in the night. I am left sleep deprived, anxious and generally have a horrible next day.

I think we're all somewhat afraid of the dark, because we don't know what is lurking out there, perhaps watching us. However, despite being a grown woman, I can't sleep without light. Even now I sleep with my lights on, because when I'm in the dark I become terrified by simple things such as a dressing gown thrown over the door, which to me resembles a demon in the room. I can't look into the dark either, without thinking about the demon waiting to attack me. It sends chills right down my spine just thinking that something might be out there, watching and lurking.

Creeks... oh, how I hate creeks! Most people think creeks are natural and beautiful, and many would love to own a cute little house beside a creek. But I know different, because I believe that wetlands are a magnet for demons. Even if I happen to drive past a creek, I become filled with anxiety and have difficulty breathing. Because of my experiences, I vow never to live near or on a creek again since I just don't know what demon is lurking there.

Another trigger for PTSD are nightmares. I have so many nightmares it's unbelievable, even when I do manage to get some sleep. Most nights my sleep is interrupted by visions of demons, with some so vivid that I wake up crying or screaming. Sometimes I dream of my grandad holding me in spirit form and reassuring me, which is helpful. But my sleep is seldom peaceful because it's exhausting to be woken up by horrible flashbacks and nightmares.

However, if demons or their followers do revisit, I will be armed with my newfound strength. As hard as it is to admit, it's difficult to truly express the way I feel to others with regard to these paranormal activities. It makes me feel alone, as if nobody else understands what I've been through. It's painful reliving those moments and talking about them. However, like I said, I want to help others. I want other people to know that they are not alone and if you are going through this experience, it can end. You can harness the power. Never let an evil spirit entity win, that's not the way it has to end.

A consequence of my terrifying experiences was being diagnosed with PTSD, which although helpful in knowing that certain treatments and therapies were available, could never be a cure. What was important was how could I heal my soul, not just my PTSD?

I never want to push my religion on anyone, and if it's not something you believe in, then that's fine, but Jesus has been a huge healing factor in my life. He has guided me along a potentially fatal path and has given me the strength to know I can handle anything that goes wrong in my life. Praying regularly has also helped me lead a better, more beautiful and demon-free life.

In our modern society, we often expect quick fixes for health problems. Western medicine focuses on curing people through surgery, pharmaceuticals and other medical interventions. Nowadays, a bacterial infection is curable with antibacterial medicines. These treatments generally focus on curing symptoms, which can be beneficial in acute situations. However, long-term reliance on treatments can also inhibit healing, creating a dependence on the treatment, which leads to additional illness and disease. For example, antibacterial medications often create an imbalance in the gut.

However, healing goes beyond just medical treatment. It includes spiritual growth, intellectual expansion, physical cures and other interventions. Healing requires digging deeper into why you experienced something in the first place, in a physical, mental or emotional sense.

Regain power. In shamanic cultures, it is important to be full of power. Power gives us the ability to be the authors of our life, rather than a character being directed by others. One way to restore power to a person, family or community, is through asking for the assistance of spirit guides, and remember to keep your mind in a happy place since it's where we spend most of our time. Positive things happen to positive people.

It's worthwhile knowing that there is no good or bad energy, but sometimes it gets misplaced. This energy often gets stuck and simply needs to be moved. The energy practices you adopt will help with this. However, it can be helpful to have a shamanic practitioner assist you to move energy that has been misplaced in your body.

Retrieve lost soul parts. When we experience trauma in life, a part of us leaves to protect us from experiencing the trauma to its full extent. This is called soul loss and a soul retrieval is a shamanic method for bringing back lost soul parts so that we may be whole again.

Reconnect with your ancestors by standing on the shoulders of others. It is important to be rooted with this, otherwise we risk becoming ruthless. Being connected to our ancestors, family and friends who love us is critical to all medicine stories. Ancestral healing, with ancestors who have passed on in the last 100 years, often helps physical issues that won't resolve themselves.

Healing with spiritual light is a cross-cultural spiritual healing technique that helps transmute negativity and toxins within and around us. As your body, heart and mind come more into balance and harmony, removing stones that have accumulated in your bowl of light over time, you find that you can hold your core in a strong, energy-filled way. You can walk through life filled with light, shining bright and inspiring others to be in their best light more and more!

Remember that meditating is another important aspect of healing your soul. It allows you the space to rejuvenate your soul, which if you're like me, sleeping won't really help. So, it's important that you take the time to breathe, relax and be off guard for a few minutes each day. This will help you feel more relaxed, more energised and stronger.

Healing sounds or frequencies may also be very beneficial for mending the soul. Healing sounds or frequencies in the form of music or binaural beats are played in a specific frequency, just as our bodies emit energy at a certain frequency. These sounds make our brain waves change frequency. When you're going through a traumatic event, our brainwave activity is usually of a frequency that is too high, meaning we're overly alert. This is necessary for moments where we need to be alert.

However, for sustained periods of time, it can be damaging to the body. Healing sounds and frequencies help lower your brainwaves to a point where you become relaxed, and your body and mind are provided with an environment to heal itself. These frequencies can be found in some music, binaural beats or instruments such as gongs and singing bowls.

There are six main frequencies that you can listen to as binaural beats, which are called Solfeggio frequencies. The unique tones and chants are found to impart spiritual blessings when they are played harmoniously. Every Solfeggio tone comprises of frequencies necessary for balancing energy, and keeping the spirit, mind and body in harmony. The following are the six main frequencies:

- The 396 Hz for liberating one from fear and guilt
- The 417 Hz frequencies for facilitating change and undoing situations
- The 528 Hz for miracles and transformations, like DNA repair
- The 639 Hz frequencies for relationships and reconnecting
- The 741 Hz for getting solutions and expressing yourself
- The 852 Hz frequencies for returning one to a spiritual order

Another obvious technique for healing is to immerse yourself in nature, go for a walk or stand in front of the ocean. Become a tree hugger or give some heartfelt affection to an animal. All these activities are calming, healing and will strengthen your soul and keep it aligned. The objective of this activity is to create a robust auric field so other bad energy can't penetrate it.

Finally, maintaining a healthy body is vital for the soul. The more physically fit you become, the stronger your barrier against harmful energy entering your energy field will be. This is one of the most important aspects of keeping yourself protected since an unhealthy body becomes an easy target and a conduit for attracting negative energy.

Exercise regularly and develop positive eating habits. The state of your health plays a big part in your 'energetic' defence. This doesn't mean you have to spend every day in the gym or only eat salad, just that you should be careful of what you consume. Every time you eat, try to tune in with your body and eat what makes you feel good. Do you feel energetic or sluggish? This will indicate to you what your body doesn't like.

PTSD is a difficult affliction, especially when it is caused by paranormal experiences which can be a long, difficult journey. However, it is often a beautiful journey and there are many ways you can heal yourself and your spirit. Even though it seems unfair, these experiences help us become who we were meant to be and walk the path we were meant to take. We need to remember that these experiences serve to make us stronger. If paranormal experiences didn't happen to me, I wouldn't be writing this book, and who knows how many people this book may help? It's important to know that there is always a bright side to pain.

CHAPTER NINETEEN

◆

Beating Trauma

People who have suffered trauma have intense, disturbing thoughts and feelings related to their experience that last long after the traumatic event has ended. They may relive the event through flashbacks or nightmares, or feel sadness, fear or anger, and they may feel detached or estranged from other people. People with trauma may evade situations or people that remind them of the event, and they may have strong negative reactions to something as innocent as a loud noise. This does depend on the severity of the trauma one experiences, and not everyone who experiences trauma suffers to this extent.

This book is all about helping people who have experienced similar episodes, or those that may come across something traumatic in the future. Although it has become easier for me, it's important to note that I am not completely healed and perhaps never will be, but a few critical steps brought me back into a more normal world.

Finding professional help is important as it could provide help if you experience trauma. Psychiatrists and other mental health professionals use various effective and research-proven methods to help people recover from trauma. Both talk therapy (psychotherapy) and medication provide effective evidence-based treatments for recovering from trauma. Psychotherapy, including cognitive behaviour therapy, can help control symptoms and help prevent them from getting worse and developing into PTSD.

However, because of paranormal activity, trauma is even more difficult to conquer because the spiritual world is something that no psychiatrist, medications or spiritualist can ever eliminate. It's always going to be there. Therefore, forgetting that a demon was ever in your home or a part of your soul is almost impossible, since they are never far away. Their very nature is to always watch out for the next weak soul to attack, or return to one that they have already attacked, knowing they always have the potential to become weak and vulnerable again.

I will never rid myself of this type of fear, and all I can do is be focused on remaining strong, positive and continue praying for protection since it has worked and served me and my family well so far. The question is... will I ever truly beat trauma? I'm not hopeful, but I am doing my best and I will never again surrender or be possessed by any demon or the devil himself. While remembering that strength does not come from winning, every struggle develops a new found strength when you go through hard traumatic times and choose not to surrender. So, stay strong everybody.

CPSIA information can be obtained
at www.ICGtesting.com
Printed in the USA
LVHW081106240521
688312LV00002B/166